Contents

KU-017-526

WITHDRAWN

Introduction

The purpose of this document is to set out clearly and simply the essential points of good chart and publication maintenance – both paper and digital.

This document does not attempt to teach navigation. In the case of paper charts and publications, it is assumed that you are able to plot from the text of an Admiralty Notice to Mariners and that you know how to position the updates accurately on the chart.

For the purpose of demonstrating paper chart updating techniques, the examples shown are from charts that were updated by hand in the UK Hydrographic Office.

SECTION ONE -

PAPER PRODUCTS

Chapter 1

How to obtain your Admiralty Notices to Mariners

In the interests of safety, it is important that Admiralty products are kept up-to-date. Access to Admiralty Notices to Mariners (NMs) can be obtained in a number of ways:

a. Printed copies are available from Admiralty Chart Agents. For details of these, see the Catalogue of Admiralty Charts and Publications (NP131), the United Kingdom Hydrographic Office (UKHO) website www.ukho.gov.uk or contact the UKHO Customer Service Desk (see below).

b. All standard Admiralty NM products are available through the UKHO website – www.ukho.gov.uk/msi. There are no subscription fees for access to this website.

Current and historical NM information (from January 2003) can be found on the UKHO website www.ukho.gov.uk/msi. This includes the full text of Weekly NM bulletins and full colour blocks and notes, and is normally updated by 1600 (UTC) on the Monday of each week (ten days before the paper version is available). For NMs prior to 2003, the Cumulative List of Notices to Mariners (NP234) must be used; this is issued every 6 months.

NM tracings are not available from the website but can be supplied electronically or in paper form by Admiralty Chart Agents.

Electronic Courier Services

The UKHO has also appointed Electronic Courier Service Providers to supply updates to Admiralty paper and digital products. Such providers supply update services, customised to the portfolio of charts and publications held on board, to vessels whilst on passage that are distributed through electronic communication channels. They also offer value added services for Admiralty; details are available from the UKHO website www.ukho.gov.uk.

UKHO Customer Service

If you experience any difficulties, please contact UKHO Customer Services on:

Tel: +44 (0)1823 337900 (24/7)

email: customerservices@ukho.gov.uk

Chapter 2

Information available from the Weekly Edition of Admiralty Notices to Mariners.

Section I Explanatory Notes. Publications List

Guidance Notes for the use of Admiralty Notices to Mariners on the UKHO Website

The beginning of Section I contains guidance notes for the use of Admiralty Notices to Mariners on the UKHO website.

Explanatory Notes, Cautionary Notes

There are a number of explanatory and cautionary notes about specific items within the Weekly Notices to Mariners. It is strongly recommended that these are thoroughly read.

Publications List

At the beginning of the Publications List is an index of Admiralty Charts affected by the Publications List. Thereafter there are a number of standard sections (outlined below) and finally any "one-off" announcements.

> ***Admiralty Charts and Publications Now Published and Available.*** This part contains a list of New Admiralty Charts and Publications, followed by New Editions of Admiralty Charts and Publications published in the last week and available from Admiralty Chart Agents. It is important to monitor this information to avoid being left with a chart which has been cancelled. When you receive a New Chart or New Edition, you must destroy any old copies immediately; it is dangerous to use a cancelled chart.

> ***Admiralty Charts and Publications to be Published.*** This is a list of charts to be published as New Charts or New Editions of existing charts and a list of new Admiralty publications scheduled to be published on a certain date in the future; these will be available from Admiralty Chart Agents on the date stated. This is included so that advanced orders may be placed with an Admiralty Chart Agent.

> ***Revised publication dates.*** This paragraph revises, if necessary, the publication date of a chart or publication which has been announced in previous weeks.

> ***Admiralty Charts and Publications Permanently Withdrawn.*** As a result of the publication of a New Chart or new publication, certain other charts or publications may be cancelled and withdrawn. It is important that the cancelled copies are destroyed as soon as you receive the new copy.

> ***Admiralty Raster Chart Service - Latest Issue Dates of Regional Discs.*** As well as the last issue date, the intended re-issue date is promulgated for regional discs due to be superseded in the near future.

> From time to time there will be a paragraph entitled ***Revised UK Recommended Retail Prices (UK RRP)*** - this will advise you of the latest revised prices of Admiralty Charts and Publications and the date these will take effect.

> Also from time to time, there will be an announcement under the heading ***Admiralty Chart Agent Information*** to show the appointment of new Admiralty Chart Agents, the termination of appointments and any changes in the address or contact details.

> ***Erratum.*** Occasionally, at the end of Section I, corrections to textual errors which have occurred in earlier Weekly Editions of Admiralty Notices to Mariners will appear.

Section IA Temporary and Preliminary (T&P) Notices (included Monthly)

This section contains a list of T&P Notices cancelled during the previous month and a list of those T&P Notices previously published and still in force.

Section IB Current Nautical Publications (included Quarterly)

Information is provided about Nautical Publications at the end of March, June, September and December. This section lists the current editions of:

- Admiralty Sailing Directions;
- Admiralty List of Lights and Fog Signals;
- Admiralty List of Radio Signals;
- Admiralty Tidal Publications; and
- Admiralty Digital Publications.

This information is also contained in the Cumulative List of Admiralty Notices to Mariners (NP234) published every six months.

Section II Admiralty Notices to Mariners. Updates to Standard Nautical Charts

Geographical Index. This index gives you a quick reference to those pages dealing with updates to charts in a particular geographical area.

Index Pages. On receipt of the Weekly Edition you should look at the Index of Charts Affected and compare it with your charts held to identify those charts to be updated. The appropriate NM numbers should be inserted against the affected chart in the Paper Chart Maintenance Record (NP133A) or other record as explained in Chapter 4. NMs are printed in numerical order within geographical regions; the Index of Notices and Chart Folios on the previous page will identify the appropriate page number for a particular NM. Some Admiralty Chart Agents/Distributors can supply lists of NM numbers tailored to your charts held on board.

Chart Updates. The first Notice in Section II refers to Miscellaneous Updates to Charts. These updates normally arise as consequential action to overlapping or different scale charts on publication of a New Chart or New Edition. For example, new chart limits may have to be inserted on a smaller scale chart covering the same area as the New Chart, or limits deleted if a chart has been cancelled. Alternatively, cautionary notes may need to be inserted or the wording altered.

Temporary and Preliminary NMs. These are shown by (T) or (P) after the NM number and before the reference to the year of publication. The explanatory notes at the beginning of Section I of the Weekly Edition include further explanation. Temporary Notices may be issued to warn of temporary changes in aids to navigation or to warn of hazards of a temporary nature e.g. a naval exercise, exploratory drilling, dredging, etc.

A Preliminary of Notice is issued to promulgate navigationally significant data early to the mariner when:

- Action/work will shortly be taking place (e.g. harbour developments; installation of, or alterations to, important navigational aids).

- Information has been received, but is too complex or extensive to be promulgated by chart updating NM. A précis of the overall changes, together with detailed navigationally significant information, will be provided in the (P) NM, with a statement that full details will be included in a New Chart or New Edition to be published shortly.

- Further confirmation of details is needed. A chart-updating NM will be promulgated, or NE issued, when the details have been confirmed.

- For ongoing and changeable situations such as a bridge construction across a major waterway. The (P) NM may be revised and reissued for updates (including diagrams if useful) as work progresses. A chart-updating NM will be promulgated, or NE issued, when the work is complete.

These Notices are placed at the end of Section II and printed only on one side of the page so that they can be cut out and pasted in a notebook or loose leaf folder for easy reference.

The information contained in T & P Notices is important navigational information which should be noted on your in-use charts in pencil. The number of the NM should also be inserted in pencil against the affected chart number in NP133A. A monthly list is published which lists all T & P Notices in force (see Section 1A above).

At the end of Section II, you will find cautionary notes, NM Blocks, depth tables and diagrams associated with the updates listed in Section II.

Section III Reprints of NAVAREA I Navigational Warnings

See the note at the start of Section III of the Weekly Edition. Information included in this Section is:

- a list of the numbers of all NAVAREA I warnings in force;
- a table of all NAVAREA I warnings issued since the last Weekly Edition, with the full text of those that were in force at the time the table was compiled.
- the full text of all NAVAREA I warnings in force is reproduced in Weekly Editions 1, 13, 26 and 39 each year.

It is recommended that in force warnings should be plotted on in-use charts in pencil and kept in a file or logbook.

More details on the World-Wide Navigational Warning Service can be found in the Mariner's Handbook (NP100) and the Admiralty List of Radio Signals Volumes 3 & 5 (NP283(1), NP283(2) & NP285)

Section IV Updates to Admiralty Sailing Directions.

Admiralty Sailing Directions (SDs) are complementary to the chart and to other navigational publications; it is important, therefore, to have a system whereby any updates can be easily retrieved and cross referenced to the particular section of the parent publication. For further details, see Chapter 6.

Section V Updates to Admiralty List of Lights and Fog Signals

Each week there are changes affecting the volumes of Admiralty List of Lights and Fog Signals (ALL). The most important of these changes are reflected in the chart updates but not necessarily in the same Weekly Edition. For further details, see Chapter 6.

Section VI Updates to Admiralty List of Radio Signals

Equally important is the information contained in the Admiralty List of Radio Signals (ALRS). Updates should be carried out in the same manner as those in the Admiralty List of Lights and Fog Signals. For further details, see Chapter 6.

Section VII Updates to Miscellaneous Admiralty Nautical Publications

Updates to selected miscellaneous Admiralty Nautical Publications are given in Section VII (see Section I of Weekly Bulletin for list of Publications).

Hydrographic Note

At the end of each Weekly Edition a Hydrographic Note (H102), a Hydrographic Note for Port Information (H102A) and a Hydrographic Note for GPS Observations Against Corresponding Admiralty Chart Positions (H102B) are included for your use should you find any information of navigational importance which is not already on your chart.

Chapter 3

Notices to Mariners - format of Chart Updates

The text of a chart updating Notice always follows the same format:

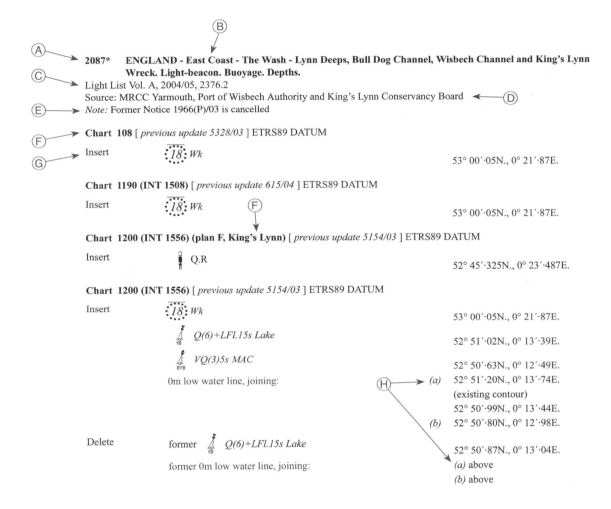

Ⓐ → **2087*** **ENGLAND - East Coast - The Wash - Lynn Deeps, Bull Dog Channel, Wisbech Channel and King's Lynn** ← Ⓑ
Wreck. Light-beacon. Buoyage. Depths.
Ⓒ → Light List Vol. A, 2004/05, 2376.2
Source: MRCC Yarmouth, Port of Wisbech Authority and King's Lynn Conservancy Board ← Ⓓ
Ⓔ → *Note:* Former Notice 1966(P)/03 is cancelled

Ⓕ → **Chart 108** [*previous update 5328/03*] ETRS89 DATUM
Ⓖ → Insert   *18* Wk   53° 00′·05N., 0° 21′·87E.

Chart 1190 (INT 1508) [*previous update 615/04*] ETRS89 DATUM
Insert   *18* Wk   Ⓕ   53° 00′·05N., 0° 21′·87E.

Chart 1200 (INT 1556) (plan F, King's Lynn) [*previous update 5154/03*] ETRS89 DATUM
Insert   Q.R   52° 45′·325N., 0° 23′·487E.

Chart 1200 (INT 1556) [*previous update 5154/03*] ETRS89 DATUM
Insert   *18* Wk   53° 00′·05N., 0° 21′·87E.

            Q(6)+LFl.15s Lake   52° 51′·02N., 0° 13′·39E.

            VQ(3)5s MAC   52° 50′·63N., 0° 12′·49E.

            0m low water line, joining: Ⓗ → (a) 52° 51′·20N., 0° 13′·74E.
                                                    (existing contour)
                                                    52° 50′·99N., 0° 13′·44E.
                                              (b)   52° 50′·80N., 0° 12′·98E.

Delete   former   Q(6)+LFl.15s Lake
                                                    52° 50′·87N., 0° 13′·04E.
            former 0m low water line, joining: (a) above
                                                    (b) above

A   The NM number in the current year which should be recorded in the bottom left hand corner of each chart after you have updated the chart. An asterisk immediately following the NM number indicates that the Notice is based on original information.

B   The title includes the geographical area or country, a more specific region or port and the nature of the update.

C   When the update affects a light and/or radio signal, the relevant Admiralty List of Lights and Fog Signals and/or Admiralty List of Radio Signals volume/edition and the appropriate entry reference will be shown.

D   The source of the information is shown under the title of the NM.

E   Occasionally an informative Note is included. These notes may be used to indicate such things as a T or P NM being cancelled by the promulgation of that particular chart update; when other charts affected by the source information will be updated in due course e.g. by Block or New Edition; or when the NM affects "Certain Copies only." "Certain Copies only" means that some copies of the charts affected have already been updated for information contained in the NM. You should plot the NM using normal procedures to determine whether your copy of the chart requires updating manually. You must always write the number of the Notice to Mariners in the bottom left hand corner of the chart even when your chart already contains the information reported in the NM.

F   The NM individually lists each chart affected, showing the relevant part or parts of the update which affect that chart.

The following points should be noted:

• Charts are listed in numerical order within each update.

• If the previous update information contained in the square brackets does not agree with the information on your chart, you are missing one or more NMs or you are using a cancelled edition. You should always insert the missing NM content onto the chart before updating it for the latest NM.

• The geodetic datum is shown alongside the chart number after "previous update". If the Notice affects a plan or inset, this is indicated.

G   The text of the update comes next. Be careful when noting positions. Positions are normally given in degrees, minutes and decimals of a minute, but may occasionally quote seconds for convenience when plotting from the graduation of some charts. In a few circumstances it will be necessary to plot using bearing and distance from charted features.

H   Positions may be cross-referenced in this manner.

Miscellaneous Updates to Charts

Miscellaneous updates primarily include changes to charts as a result of the publication of the New Editions and New Charts listed in Section I. These can include changes to the limits of larger scale charts, changed "adjoining chart" references or altered cautionary notes. The following is an example of a Miscellaneous Update:

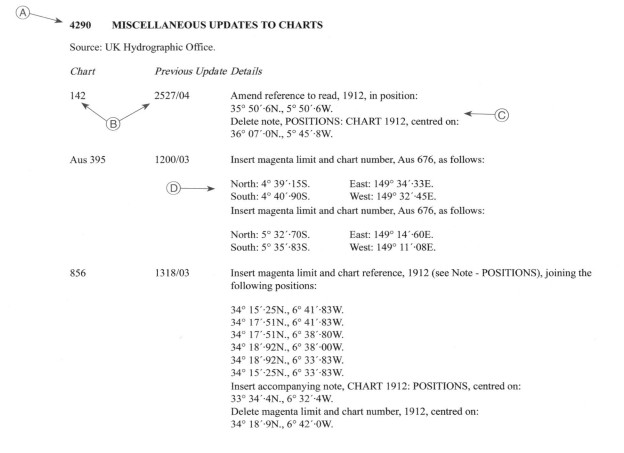

4290   MISCELLANEOUS UPDATES TO CHARTS

Source: UK Hydrographic Office.

Chart	Previous Update	Details
142	2527/04	Amend reference to read, 1912, in position: 35° 50'·6N., 5° 50'·6W. Delete note, POSITIONS: CHART 1912, centred on: 36° 07'·0N., 5° 45'·8W.
Aus 395	1200/03	Insert magenta limit and chart number, Aus 676, as follows: North: 4° 39'·15S. East: 149° 34'·33E. South: 4° 40'·90S. West: 149° 32'·45E. Insert magenta limit and chart number, Aus 676, as follows: North: 5° 32'·70S. East: 149° 14'·60E. South: 5° 35'·83S. West: 149° 11'·08E.
856	1318/03	Insert magenta limit and chart reference, 1912 (see Note - POSITIONS), joining the following positions: 34° 15'·25N., 6° 41'·83W. 34° 17'·51N., 6° 41'·83W. 34° 17'·51N., 6° 38'·80W. 34° 18'·92N., 6° 38'·00W. 34° 18'·92N., 6° 33'·83W. 34° 15'·25N., 6° 33'·83W. Insert accompanying note, CHART 1912: POSITIONS, centred on: 33° 34'·4N., 6° 32'·4W. Delete magenta limit and chart number, 1912, centred on: 34° 18'·9N., 6° 42'·0W.

A   The miscellaneous NM number in the current year which should be recorded in the bottom left hand corner of each chart updated. The miscellaneous NM update is always the first Notice to appear in Section II of the weekly.

B   The chart to be updated and the previous update number.

C   The text of the update to be applied.

D   The instruction to insert new larger-scale chart limits is shown like this. Draw a "box" with these limits and insert the chart number (in this case Aus 676) in a corner of the box clear of other detail.

Chapter 4

Equipment - Tools

It is recommended that you have the proper tools before you begin to update your charts.

1. **Pens** You need two pens with different sizes of nib - use a 0.18mm nib to insert information and a 0.25mm nib to delete.

2. **Ink** Always use violet ink so that your updates can be clearly seen, since red ink disappears under the red lighting frequently used at night[1]. Updates will then also be clearly visible to Port State, Flag State, Class and Insurance surveyor inspection teams. The use of violet ink is also appropriate for applying updates to charts printed with multiple colours including, for example, coloured light sector bands and light flare symbols. Attempting to replicate the colour of the printed chart in applying updates is not recommended.

3. **Pencils** A 7H is suggested for pin-pointing positions when using either a parallel rule and dividers or a tracing. For normal chart work mariners may prefer a softer pencil such as a 2B.

4. **Eraser** This should be soft and used only for rubbing out pencil marks or tracks on charts or Notices to Mariners (NMs) recorded in the Paper Chart Maintenance Record (NP133A).

5. **Adhesive** A firm adhesive must be used when sticking NM Blocks and notes onto charts to ensure that there is no distortion to the chart or the Block. There are many types of firm positionable mounting adhesive rolls on the market and it is important to use one which provides a permanent fixing.

6. **Parallel rule** There are two types – rolling and stepping; both are perfectly suitable for the purpose of plotting chart updates.

7. **Dividers** Bow dividers are more sensitive for accurate positioning.

8. **Compass** With a pen attachment; this is an essential piece of equipment for updating where you have to draw large circles or sectors.

9. **Hacksaw blade** A useful tool which you can use to draw the symbol for a cable. The blade should have about 14 teeth to 1 inch (2.5cm). Be careful to use the blade so that the pen will flow over the teeth.

10. **Straight edge** A steel straight edge, preferably 1 metre in length with a true and straight edge, is a useful tool for finding a position on a chart. It is a slower process than using a parallel rule and dividers but there is less room for error.

11. **Template** With various sizes of holes; used for drawing symbols for radar beacons, small circular limits, etc.

---

[1] Use of correcting fluid or tape should be avoided, since these may flake or peel during use.

Equipment - Publications

12. **NP133A**

Paper Chart Maintenance Record. This publication may be purchased from any appointed Admiralty Chart Agent; it lists every chart numerically and is used to record updates (by their NM number) against any chart affected. It is recommended that, when the Admiralty NMs are received, you should identify those charts which are affected and immediately record the relevant NM number against the chart number in NP133A. You can update your charts later and cross the appropriate NM number through in NP133A as you complete each update. The date of the New Edition/New Chart should be entered in ink as a permanent record. The year date for the current year of NMs should be underlined so that it is not confused with an NM number.

Extract from Paper Chart Maintenance Record (NP133A)

Chart No.	Folio No.	Notices to Mariners affecting chart
3061	89	1987 OCT 2 (NE)-2002-117-2127-5172-5435-2003-2343-2973
3062	11	1990 DEC 21 (NE)-2002-429-559-783-5475-2003-756

You may prefer to use a lined jotter or note book with a list of the chart numbers in numerical order; a card index system based on folio content; or a computer spreadsheet program.

Whichever system is used, it is vital that an up-to-date record is maintained of all updates affecting all charts held. Without such a record it is very easy to lose track of where you are in the updating process. If this happens, the process will become chaotic and you are likely to miss NMs.

13. **NP234**

Cumulative List of Admiralty Notices to Mariners, published twice a year. The first is published in January and includes all NM numbers published during the previous two years. The July edition includes all the NM numbers published during the previous two and a half years. It also contains the latest edition dates for all charts in the Admiralty series. It is a very useful tool for checking the accuracy of your record of updates. It is the only source of information when setting up an NM record system for the first time. The list can also be found on the UKHO website at: www.ukho.gov.uk/msi

14. **NP5011**

Symbols and Abbreviations used on Admiralty Charts is based on the Chart Specifications of the International Hydrographic Organization (IHO) adopted in 1982, with later additions and updates. The layout and numbering accords with the official IHO version of INT 1. It explains every symbol used on Admiralty Charts and should be used as a guide during the chart updating process. It is updated by NM in Section VII of the Weekly Admiralty Notices to Mariners when necessary.

15.	'X' Charts	When important changes to routeing measures or other charted features are due to come into force on a given day, it is important that chart users are aware of the changes before the event takes place. Sometimes the safest and easiest way to promulgate these changes is to issue a New Edition of the chart in advance of the changeover day, with the new details depicted. This chart will then be readily available for use when the changeover occurs. However, until that date, mariners should continue to use the existing edition of the chart.

To stop the existing and updated charts becoming confused, the UKHO refers to the existing chart as an 'X' chart. Mariners are instructed to mark the chart number on the existing chart with a prefix 'X'. Both charts will then need to be kept up-to-date until the New Edition comes into force, at which time the 'X' chart will be cancelled. Separate updates will be issued for the New Edition and the 'X' chart. (Only (T) NMs will be issued to update the 'X' chart.) The date and time that the New Edition comes into force will be shown on the chart.

16.	NP247	**The Annual Summary of Admiralty Notices to Mariners** is published in two parts in January each year. Part 1 contains the text of Annual Notices to Mariners issued in that year and a reprint of all Temporary and Preliminary Notices to Mariners in force at the beginning of the year. Part 2 contains a reprint of updates to Admiralty Sailing Directions and Miscellaneous Nautical Publications that have been issued since publication of the latest editions or supplements. These books are an essential part of a chart outfit; you should make sure that you have them on board as soon as they have been published, and replace them annually. They can also be downloaded from the UKHO website.

17.	NP131	Catalogue of Admiralty Charts and Publications - see Chapter 6.

How to apply the updates to your charts

All NMs should be recorded against the appropriate chart number in NP133A. Thereafter all charts in current use and those required for any forthcoming passage should be updated immediately; other charts held on board should then be updated as time allows.

Where more than one copy of a chart is held, either each copy should be recorded separately in NP133A or a pencil notation should be made against the chart number indicating how many copies are held. It is important that all copies are maintained consistently so as to avoid the possibility of a copy that has not been updated being used.

The principles, practices and conventions of chart updating are illustrated by the examples in Chapter 5. Though reference is made to the tracing in the examples given, always refer to the Admiralty Notice to Mariners text which is the primary source. By reading the NM whilst looking at the chart in question you will avoid the risk of deleting information which otherwise could have been used to complement the new information being inserted.

Violet ink should be used for applying all updates including those charts printed with multiple colours including, for example, coloured light sector bands and light flare symbols. Attempting to replicate the colour of the printed chart in applying updates is not recommended.

It should be noted that a tracing is only a guide to illustrate the update and to pin-point a position. Special symbols are used on the tracing to indicate insertions and deletions; these should NOT be copied faithfully onto the chart. The following examples will point out mistakes which can be made if the information you are inserting on the chart is copied from a tracing. If tracings are used, these should be stored by chart number so that in the event of a change of passage plan any charts that are required but have not been updated can quickly be brought up-to-date. Tracings should always be filed by chart number. That way all the relevant information for any particular chart is kept together and, if that chart is cancelled or replaced by a New Edition or a New Chart, all the old tracings relating to that chart can be destroyed.

There is not an example of an NM Block. These should be aligned accurately and stuck onto the affected charts. It is important to remember to completely remove the enclosing black line around the limits of the area of a block before sticking it onto the chart; there is normally at least 5mm inside the line with no new or deleted information on it. Care should be taken that new block information does not obscure parts of previously inserted updates (for example, where a sounding has been inserted under the new block but arrowed-in to a position outside it).

The following procedure will help you avoid making mistakes:

- Using the information in the NM (in conjunction with the tracing, if you have it), apply the update to the chart.
- Check what you have done.
- When you are satisfied that you have correctly followed the instructions of the NM (and only then) write the NM number in the bottom left hand corner of the chart as a record of the completed update. It is dangerous to insert the NM number in the bottom left hand corner of the chart before you have updated the chart. The year date for the current year of NMs should be underlined so that it is not confused with an NM number
- When you have completed all the steps above, cross through the NM number adjacent to the chart in your NP133A or similar record.

Further advice can be obtained from the DVD "How to Update Admiralty Standard Nautical Charts" or by asking your Admiralty Chart Agent.

Any charts held on board that are not, and will not, be maintained up-to-date should clearly be marked "NOT TO BE USED FOR NAVIGATION".

Explanation of Terms used in Notices to Mariners

The main text of the update starts with one of the following five commands, usually in the order shown:

INSERT is used for the insertion of all new data or, together with the **DELETE** command, when a feature has moved position sufficiently that the **MOVE** command is inappropriate.

AMEND is used when a feature remains in its existing charted position but has a change of characteristic, for example:

      Amend light to, Fl.3s25m10M   32°36´·90S., 60°54´·18E.

      When only the range of a light changes:
      Amend range of light to, 10M   32°36´·90S., 60°54´·18E.

REPLACE is to be used when one feature replaces an existing, but different, feature and the position remains unchanged. The old feature will always come first in the sentence, e.g. Replace xx with yy (where yy is the new feature).

EXAMPLE

      Replace   depth *34* with depth *29*   57°44´·61N., 11°05´·97E.

MOVE is used for features whose characteristics or descriptions remain unchanged, but they are to be moved small distances, for example:

      Move   *No 3* light-buoy, from: 56°00´·62S., 4°46´·47E.

                      to: 56°00´·30S., 4°46´·35E

DELETE is used when features are to be removed from the chart or, together with the **INSERT** command, when features are moved a significant distance such that the **MOVE** command is inappropriate.

The "***Certain copies only***" informative note occasionally included in the NM means that some printed copies of the charts affected have already been updated for information contained in the NM. (The number of the NM must always be written in the bottom left hand corner of the chart even if your chart already contains the information).

Explanation of Symbols and Instructions on Tracings

Insertion: Information to be inserted will be boxed. The position of the insertion is shown as a small circle containing a dot at its centre. An arrow will be shown from the box to the circle (⊷→). Sometimes clarification may be required regarding what should be inserted or deleted. This is often the case with a replacement where words such as "in lieu" may be added to the tracing to assist those carrying out updates.

Deletion: Information to be deleted will be boxed and hatched out by diagonal lines. A deletion symbol (⌀) will be annotated next to the boxed area. Where a cautionary note is being deleted, the words "Delete + the title of the note" will be inside the hatched area.

Linear features: Short lines are used to indicate the turning points of linear features such as pipelines, cables or area limits thus: ———┴——

Plotting from Tracings on a Chart

The positioning of tracings should always be checked carefully using three methods, as follows:

- Latitude and Longitude lines shown
- Location on Chart (e.g. ⊞)
- Other fitting marks shown such as soundings or prominent features

Drawing Conventions when Updating Charts

It is good practice to observe the following conventions when updating charts:

Insertions: Do not make the common error of drawing exactly what is on the tracing onto the chart. Insertions can often be made by drawing the new feature in an open area of the chart and "arrowing it in" to a small circle in the correct position. Other insertions are shown in the exact position by drawing the feature in the correct location; a new legend is a typical example of this.

Deletions: These should be made by drawing two straight lines through each piece of text or feature to be deleted. Do not delete items in the same manner as shown on the tracings. If there is any doubt, the tracing will be annotated with amplifying information so that adjacent information, for example, is not deleted in error.

Moves: Occasionally features are moved a short distance from their original position. Draw a small circle at the new position and arrow the feature to that position.

New Symbols: The examples that follow do not contain a complete set of symbols used on tracings. New symbols may be introduced from time to time. If unsure of the meaning, always consult the text of the NM for clarification.

Replacements: Wherever possible, overwriting of existing information should be avoided; point symbols (i.e. depths, buoys, lights) should be inserted in a clear space and "arrowed" into position. Legends may be amended by inserting the new text in clear space adjacent to the existing charted detail.

Final Notes

The examples shown in this booklet are by no means exhaustive but should be sufficient to illustrate the principles involved. When you are updating your charts you should try to achieve the very highest standards of draughtsmanship so that you can read the information clearly.

Most important of all:

- Positions must be **exact**.
- Depths and symbols must be **clear**.
- Legends and descriptions must be **legible**.

Chapter 5

Examples

Example 1   Insert new buoyage

6172   AUSTRALIA - Western Australia - Port of Dampier - Parker Point Westwards - Buoyage. Depth.
Source: Australian Notice 24/1035/05
(*HH.571/009/2005-06 e35*).

Chart Aus 58 [*previous update New Edition 18/03/2005*] WGS84 DATUM

Insert	△ *Fl.Y.2·5s*		20° 38′·545S., 116° 42′·729E.
		(a)	20° 38′·462S., 116° 42′·953E.
			20° 38′·344S., 116° 43′·154E.
Delete	depth 7_1 , close SW of:		*(a)* above

Chart Aus 59 (plan, Dampier Wharves) [*previous update 3081/05*] AUSTRALIAN GEODETIC DATUM

Insert	△ *Fl.Y.2·5s B1*	*(a)*	20° 38′·624S., 116° 42′·649E.
	△ *Fl.Y.2·5s B2*		20° 38′·623S., 116° 42′·734E.
	△ *Fl.Y.2·5s B3*		20° 38′·542S., 116° 42′·873E.
	△ *Fl.Y.2·5s B4*		20° 38′·423S., 116° 43′·074E.
Delete	depth 7_4 , close W of:		*(a)* above

Notes

The most simple of updates – a straightforward addition of new buoyage. If you have access to the tracing, accurately position this over the chart and mark through the small circle showing the location of the new buoyage. Where possible, the new symbols should be drawn in the exact positions. If there is not enough space to do this, then draw a small circle on the chart at the correct position. In a clear area of the chart, draw the buoy, light description and light flare and arrow this into the circle at the new position. As with all updates, add the NM number to the bottom left-hand corner of the chart.

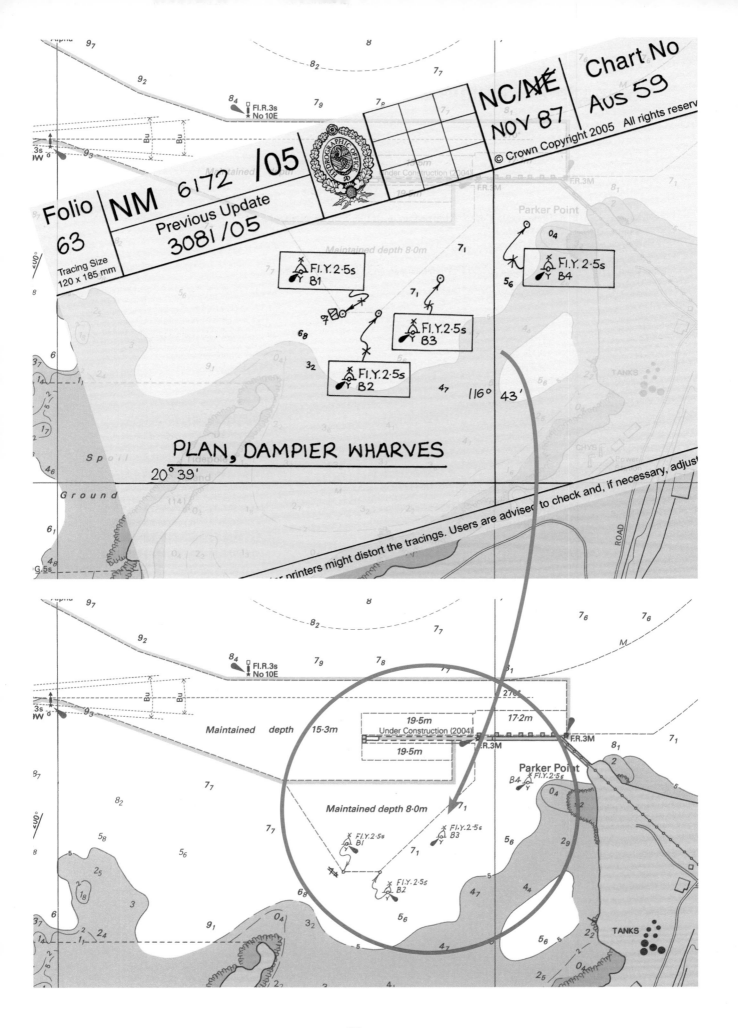

NC/NE | Chart No
NOV 87 | Aus 59

Folio | NM 6172 /05
63 | Previous Update
3081 /05

Tracing Size
120 x 185 mm

Fl.R.3s
No 10E

Fl.Y.2·5s
Y B1

Fl.Y.2·5s
Y B3

Fl.Y.2·5s
Y B2

Fl.Y.2·5s
Y B4

Maintained depth 8·0m

Parker Point

PLAN, DAMPIER WHARVES

20° 39'

116° 43'

Spoil

Ground

Maintained   depth   15·3m

19·5m
Under Construction (2004)
19·5m

17·2m

F.R.3M

F.R.3M

Maintained depth 8·0m

Parker Point

B4 Fl.Y.2·5s
Y

Fl.Y.2·5s
B1

Fl.Y.2·5s
B3

Fl.Y.2·5s
B2

TANKS

ROAD

printers might distort the tracings. Users are advised to check and, if necessary, adjust

Example 2   Delete a swept area

6029   CHINA - Yellow Sea Coast - Approaches to Dalian Xingang - Swept area.
Source: Chinese Chart 11381
(*HH.548/527/-03 e38*).

Chart 1249 [*previous update 5628/05*] UNDETERMINED DATUM

Delete	limit of swept area, pecked line, joining:	*(a)*	38° 52´·7N., 121° 58´·0E. (E border)
		(b)	38° 52´·7N., 121° 55´·2E.
		(c)	38° 55´·5N., 121° 55´·2E. (harbour limit) and
		(d)	38° 56´·8N., 121° 57´·3E. (harbour limit)
		(e)	38° 56´·8N., 121° 58´·0E. (E border)
	20, within:		*(a)-(e)* above

Chart 1255 [*previous update 5728/05*] BEIJING (1954) DATUM

Delete	limit of swept area, pecked line, joining:	*(a)*	38° 54´·9N., 121° 58´·5E.
		(b)	38° 52´·7N., 121° 58´·5E.
		(c)	38° 52´·7N., 121° 55´·2E.
		(d)	38° 55´·3N., 121° 55´·2E. (harbour limit)
	20, within:		*(a)-(d)* above

Notes

This is another simple update - the deletion of a swept area. Using a 0.25mm nib, draw two lines through the "20" depth, the symbol and the limit. The existing limit is deleted by neatly striking through as shown on the tracing. Note that the tracing shows the work to be deleted by cross-hatching. This is for clarity only and should not be copied onto the chart.

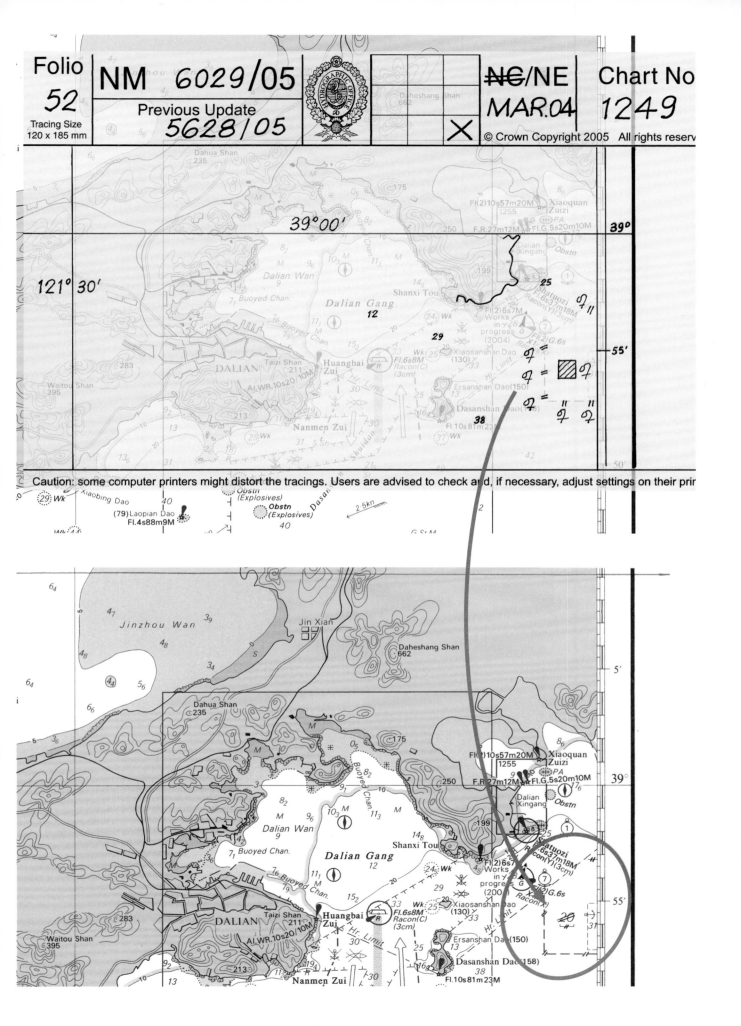

NM 6029/05
Previous Update
5628/05

NC/NE
MAR.04

Chart No
1249

39°00'

121°30'

Caution: some computer printers might distort the tracings. Users are advised to check and, if necessary, adjust settings on their pri

Example 3   Replace a buoy with a light-buoy

2877   **WEST INDIES - Windward Islands - Martinique, North East Coast - Loup Sainte-Marie - Buoy.**
Source: French Notice 18/70/06
(*HH.671/480/-05 e17*).

Chart 371 (plan C, Havre de la Trinité) [*previous update 1789/06*] SHOM 1984 DATUM

Replace   "TR1"   with   Fl.R.4s "TR1"

14° 48´·11N., 60° 59´·00W.

Chart 371 (plan, Pointe Caracoli to Fort-de-France) [*previous update 1789/06*] SHOM 1984 DATUM

Replace   "TR1"   with   Fl.R.4s "TR1"

14° 48´·11N., 60° 59´·00W.

Chart 594 [*previous update 1296/06*] WGS84 DATUM

Replace   "TR1"   with   Fl.R.4s "TR1"

14° 48´·2N., 60° 58´·8W.

Notes

In this example, one feature replaces another. Using the existing buoy, insert the light description and then add a light flare. This avoids a deletion and an insertion on the chart.

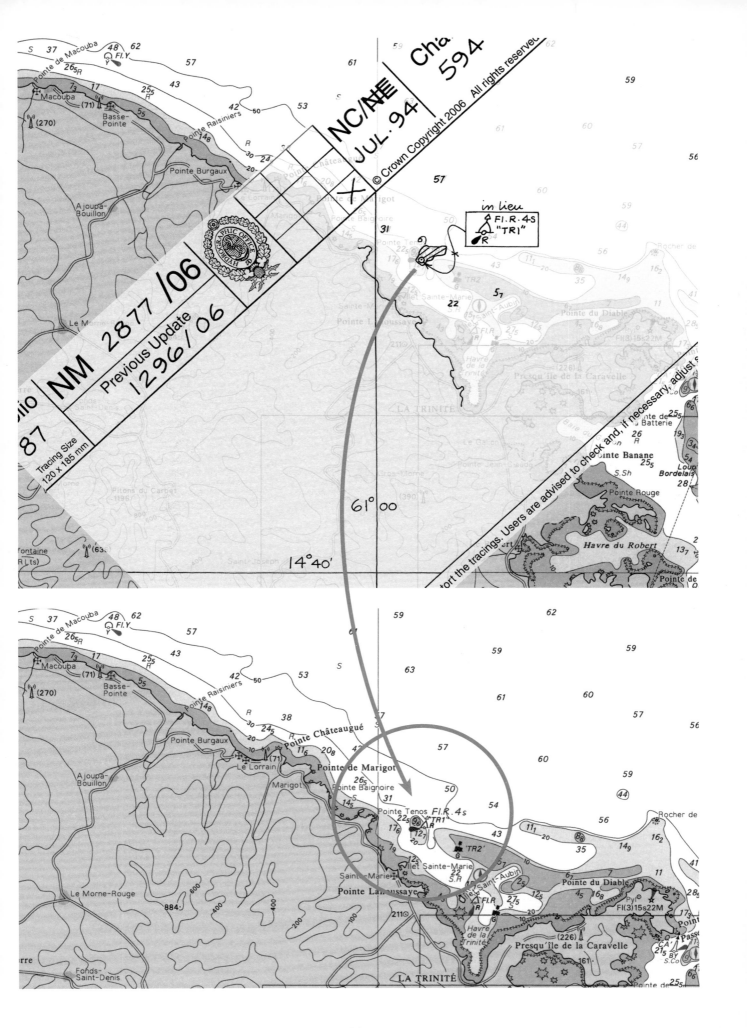

NC/NE
JUL. 94

Ch'a
594

in lieu
Fl.R.4s
"TR1"
R

NM 2877/06
Previous Update
1296/06

Tracing Size
120 x 185 mm

Example 4   Insert a light and breakwater

6009   JAPAN - Honshū - North West Coast - Toyama - Yokata - Lights. Breakwater.
Light List Vol. F, 2005/06, 7150.6
Source: Japanese Notice 48/1437/05
(*HH.563/510/-04 e40*).

Chart 1342 (plan D, Toyama) [*previous update 3227/05*] WGS84 DATUM		
Insert	☆ Fl.R.3s11m3M	*(a)* 36° 45′·71N., 137° 11′·56E.
	breakwater, single firm line, joining:	*(a)* above 36° 45′·68N., 137° 11′·50E.
Delete	☆ Fl.G.3s7m5M, close SE of:	*(a)* above

Notes

Lights must be drawn in the correct position, not arrowed in unless stated "move" in the text of the Notice. Light descriptions should always be as close to the light star as possible, but care must be taken to make sure they do not obscure other important existing information. Follow the instructions in the text and draw the light first and its flare. Then draw the breakwater joining the light to the position quoted. Although this is a single line, it should be drawn fairly heavily so that the breakwater stands out. Once the new information is in, neatly cross through the existing light, not forgetting its light description.

PLAN Ⓓ TOYAMA

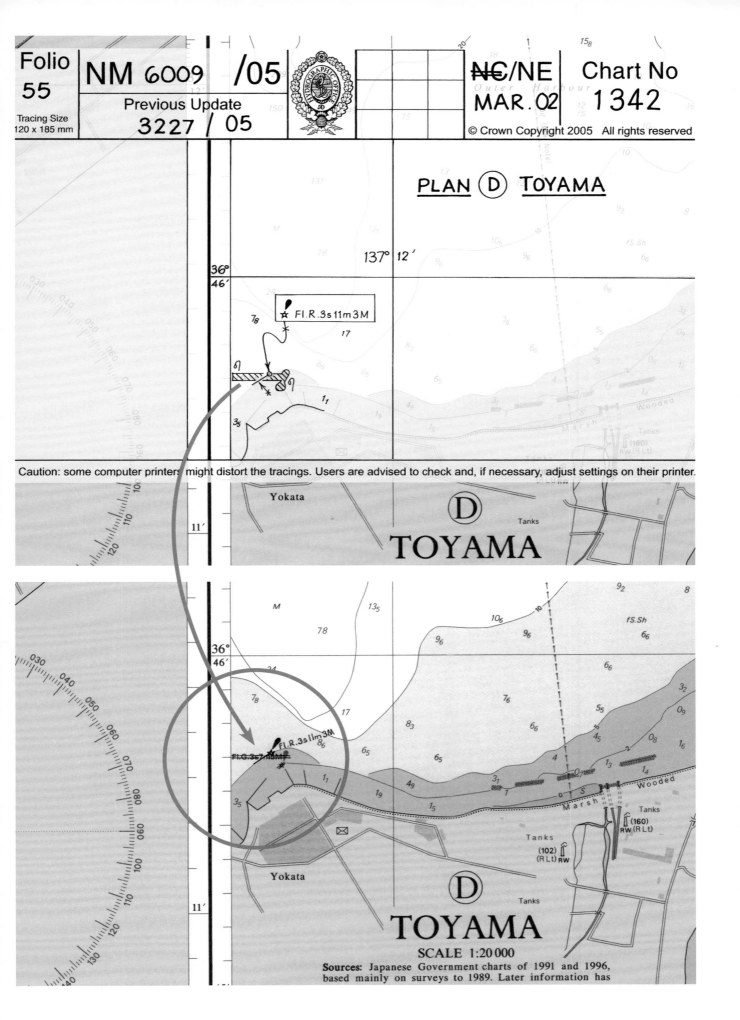

Caution: some computer printers might distort the tracings. Users are advised to check and, if necessary, adjust settings on their printer.

Yokata

Tanks

Ⓓ

TOYAMA

Yokata

Ⓓ

TOYAMA

SCALE 1:20 000

Sources: Japanese Government charts of 1991 and 1996, based mainly on surveys to 1989. Later information has

Example 5   Move a light

2653   NEW ZEALAND - North Island - East Coast - Hauraki Gulf - Motuihe Island Northwards - North Reef Point - Light.
Light List Vol. K, 2006/07, 3845.1
Source: New Zealand Notice 10/96/06
(HH.580/009/-2006 e15).

Chart NZ 532 [*previous update 307/06*] WGS84 DATUM

Move	★ Fl.R from:	36° 47′·80S., 174° 56′·20E.
	to:	36° 47′·74S., 174° 56′·25E.

Chart NZ 5324 [*previous update 307/06*] WGS84 DATUM

Move	★ Fl.R.3s3m1M from:	36° 47′·80S., 174° 56′·20E.
	to:	36° 47′·74S., 174° 56′·25E.

Notes

"Move" is used for features whose characteristics or descriptions remain unchanged, but they are to be moved small distances. Follow the instructions on the text and tracing. Draw a small circle on the chart at the new position and arrow the feature to the circle.

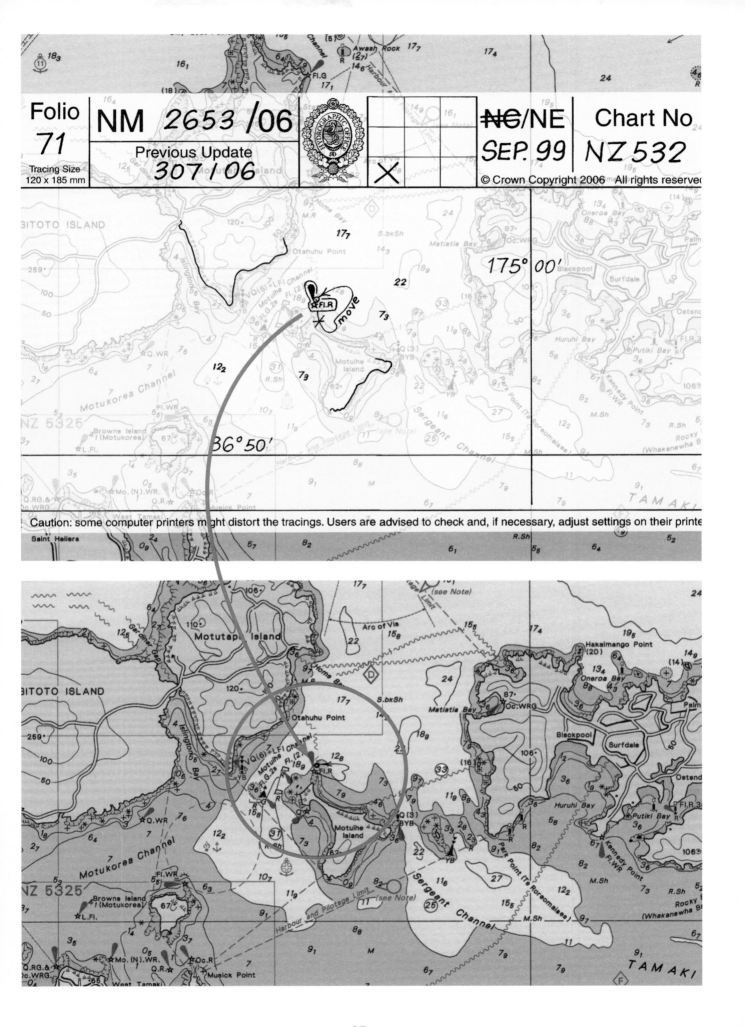

Caution: some computer printers might distort the tracings. Users are advised to check and, if necessary, adjust settings on their printe

Example 6   Replace a beacon with a light

2931   NORWAY - West Coast - Sognefjorden - Ortnevik Northwards - Beacon. Light.
Light List Vol. L, 2006/07, 0093
Source: Norwegian Notice 10/579/06
(*HH.310/465/-04 e8*).

Chart 2291 [*previous update 1137/06*] WGS84 DATUM

Replace   ⚓   with   ★ Q   61° 06′·9N., 6° 08′·3E.

Notes

This is an update where a light replaces another feature. Lights should be drawn in their correct positions unless the "move" command is used in the text of the Notice and on the tracing. Neatly draw the light star on top of the beacon it is replacing. Write the light description alongside and draw the light flare, covering the beacon as shown on the tracing.

Folio 13

NM 2931 /06

Previous Update
1137 /06

Tracing Size
120 x 185 mm

X

~~NC~~/NE
DEC.04

Chart No
2291

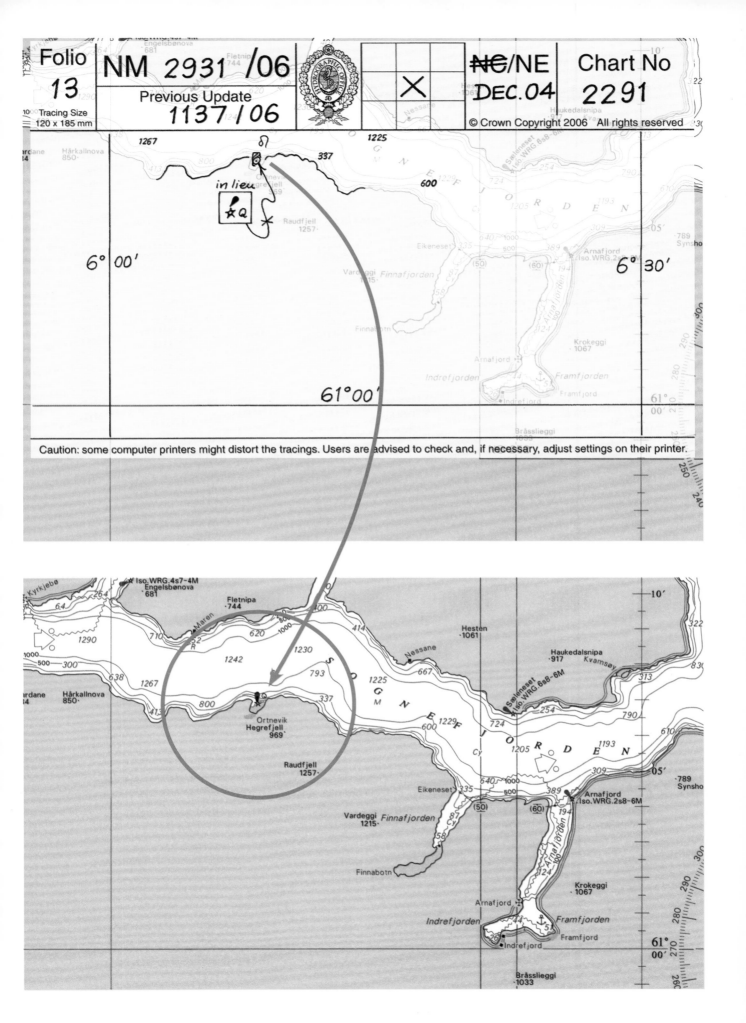

Caution: some computer printers might distort the tracings. Users are advised to check and, if necessary, adjust settings on their printer.

Example 7   Insert a pipeline and legend

**5492*   NORTH SEA - United Kingdom Sector - Buchan Oil Field North-north-eastwards - Submarine pipelines.
         Legend.**
Source: Talisman Energy (UK) Limited
(*HH.254/701/-02 e18*).
Note: Former Notice 3237(P)/05 is cancelled.

Chart 2 (INT 160) [*previous update 5491/05*] UNDETERMINED DATUM

Insert	submarine pipeline, ▸▸▸▸, joining:		
		(a)	57° 57´·0N., 0° 11´·6E.
		(b)	58° 17´·3N., 0° 09´·3E.
			58° 27´·7N., 0° 15´·0E. (⊡)
	legend, *Oil & Gas*, along:		*(a)-(b)* above

Chart 278 [*previous update 5082/05*] ED50 DATUM

Insert	submarine pipeline, ▸▸▸▸, joining:		
		(a)	57° 59´·77N., 0° 11´·71E.
			(◌ *Wells*)
		(b)	58° 01´·20N., 0° 11´·95E.
		(c)	58° 05´·60N., 0° 09´·80E.
			58° 06´·50N., 0° 10´·05E.
			58° 09´·76N., 0° 09´·51E.
			(N border)
			and
			(a) above
			57° 58´·50N., 0° 11´·00E.
			57° 57´·68N., 0° 07´·70E.
			(◌ *Well*)
			and
			57° 57´·07N., 0° 11´·72E.
			(◌ *Well*)
			57° 57´·90N., 0° 11´·40E.
			(a) above
	legend, *Oil & Gas (see Note)*, along:		*(b)-(c)* above

Notes

The tracing shows the turning points of the pipeline as short lines drawn across the symbol. Plot the positions of these or mark them through the tracing. Use a straight edge and draw the pipeline symbol, breaking it where necessary so that existing information on the chart is not obscured. Add the legend as shown on the tracing.

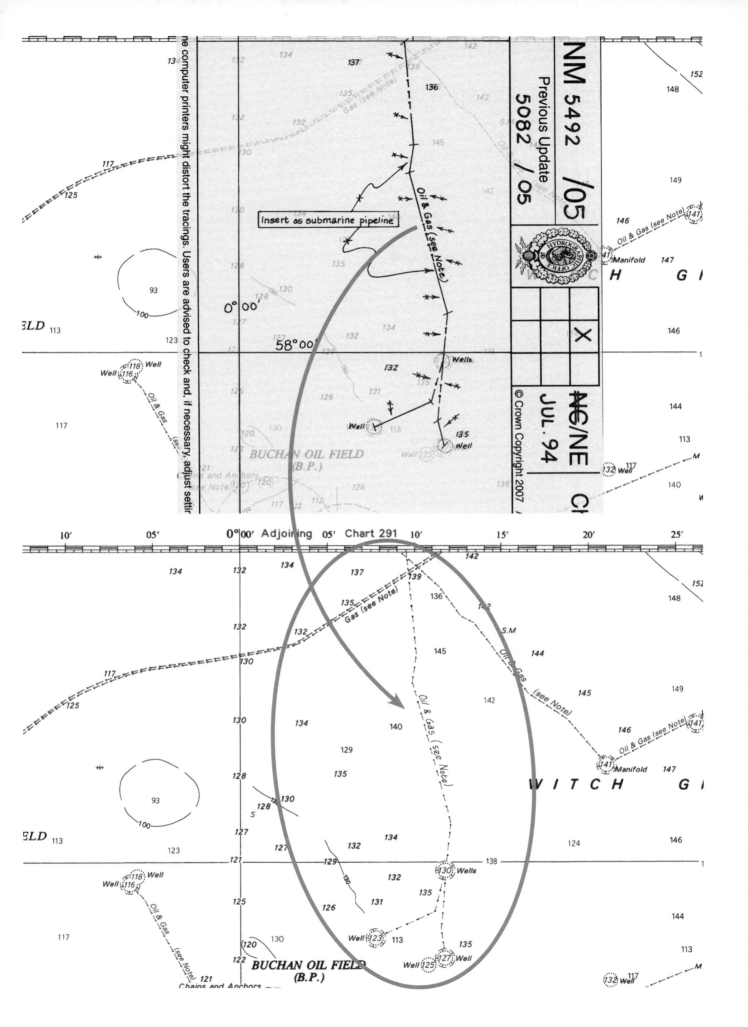

NM 5492 /05

Previous Update
5082 / 05

ne computer printers might distort the tracings. Users are advised to check and, if necessary, adjust settir

Insert as submarine pipeline

NG/NE
JUL. 94

© Crown Copyright 2007

X

0°00'

58°00'

134

137

136

142

148

152

149

146

147

Manifold

146

144

113

117

140

Oil & Gas (see Note)

Oil & Gas (see Note)

Gas (see Note)

117

125

130

132

135

134

128

93

100

JLD 113

123

Well 118

Well 116

Well

117

Oil & Gas (see Note)

120

130

122

BUCHAN OIL FIELD
(B.P.)

Chains and Anchors
(see Note)

120

128

117

112

132

131

126

125

128

130

132

134

Wells

Well 113

135

Well

Well 125

136

10'   05'   0°00' Adjoining 05' Chart 291 10'   15'   20'   25'

134   132   134   137   139   142   152

135   136   148

Gas (see Note)

S.M

132   132   130   145   144   149

117

125   130   134   129   135   140   142   145

146   141

Oil & Gas (see Note)

Oil & Gas (see Note)

141 Manifold   147

W I T C H   G I

128   93   128   130   79

S   130

100

JLD 113   127   134   124   146

123   121   127   132   138

125   129   132   135   144

126   131   135   113

Well 123   113

130   117   113

120

122   Well 125   127 Well

BUCHAN OIL FIELD
(B.P.)

Chains and Anchors

132 Well   M

130 Wells

41

Example 8   Insert a leading line

3162*   **INDONESIA - Nusatenggara - Bali - Benoa Eastwards - Light-beacon. Leading line. Legend. Buoyage. Beacons. (continued)**

Chart 946 (plan D, Approaches to Benoa) [*previous update 2312/06*] UNDETERMINED DATUM			
Move	symbol, white light-beacon with topmark, Fl.3s9M, from:	*(a)*	8° 45´·60S., 115° 13´·30E.
	to:	*(b)*	8° 45´·55S., 115° 13´·29E.
Insert	leading line, pecked line for 720m then firm line for 4850m, extending in direction 75·5° from:	*(c)*	*(b)* above
	legend, 255·5°, seaward end of:		*(c)* above
Delete	former leading line, pecked and firm line, and associated legend 250°, extending in direction 070° from:		*(a)* above

Notes

When inserting a leading line it is important to follow the instructions in the NM exactly so that the right amount of pecked and firm line is shown. This ensures that the user has a clear understanding of how these lights are used for navigation

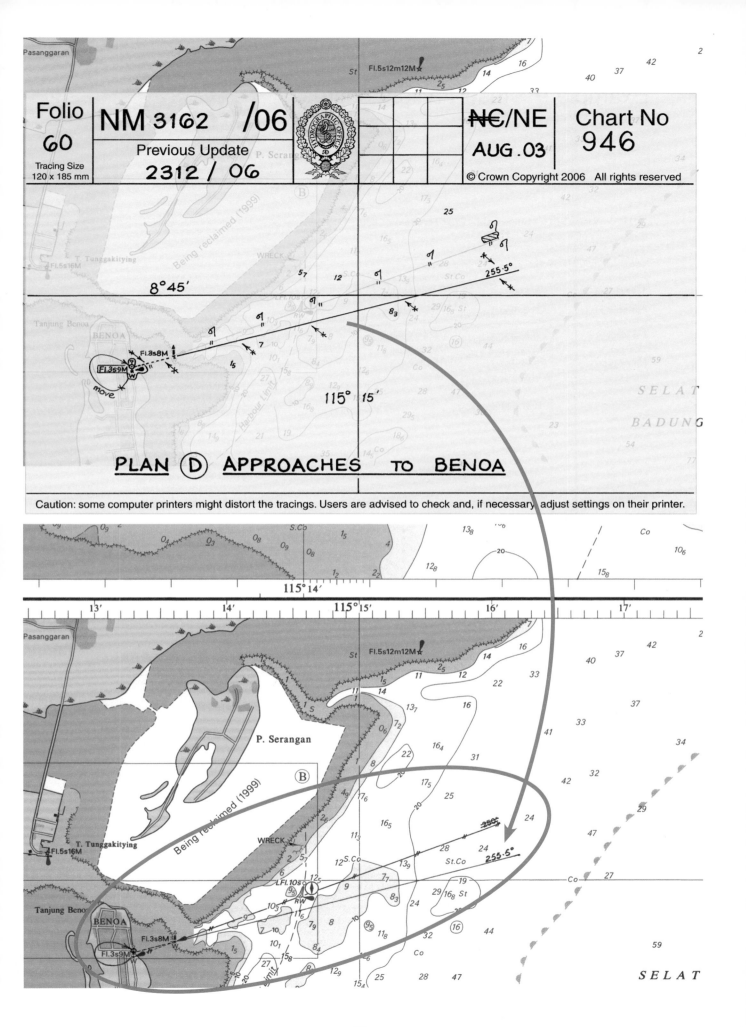

Folio 60	NM 3162 /06				~~NC~~/NE	Chart No
Tracing Size 120 x 185 mm	Previous Update 2312 / 06				AUG .03	946

Caution: some computer printers might distort the tracings. Users are advised to check and, if necessary, adjust settings on their printer.

PLAN ⒟ APPROACHES TO BENOA

43

Example 9　Insert a light sector

3211　ESTONIA - Muuga Laht - Coal Terminal - Light.
Light List Vol. C, 2006/07, 3852
Source: Estonian Notice 6/57/06
(SEP: 2006000366014).

Chart 2225 [*previous update 2100/06*] WGS84 DATUM

Insert

★ Oc.WRG.4s30m2M (Oct - May)

sectors at light as follows:
G 086° - 102°　(16°)

W 102° - 108°　(6°)

R 108° - 119°　(11°)

(a)　59° 30′·21N., 24° 59′·97E.
(a) above

Notes

This is a small light sector. Draw the light star and flare in the correct position with the description in a clear space as close as possible. Remember that bearings for lights are shown from seaward. Either plot the sectors of the light or use the tracing as a guide. For updating purposes, light sectors can be drawn as solid lines. It is good practice to use a compass to draw the arcs. Do not forget to show the colours of the sectors against the arcs.

If your chart includes coloured light flares and sectors it is acceptable to insert the sectors as described above; this avoids the need for coloured pens.

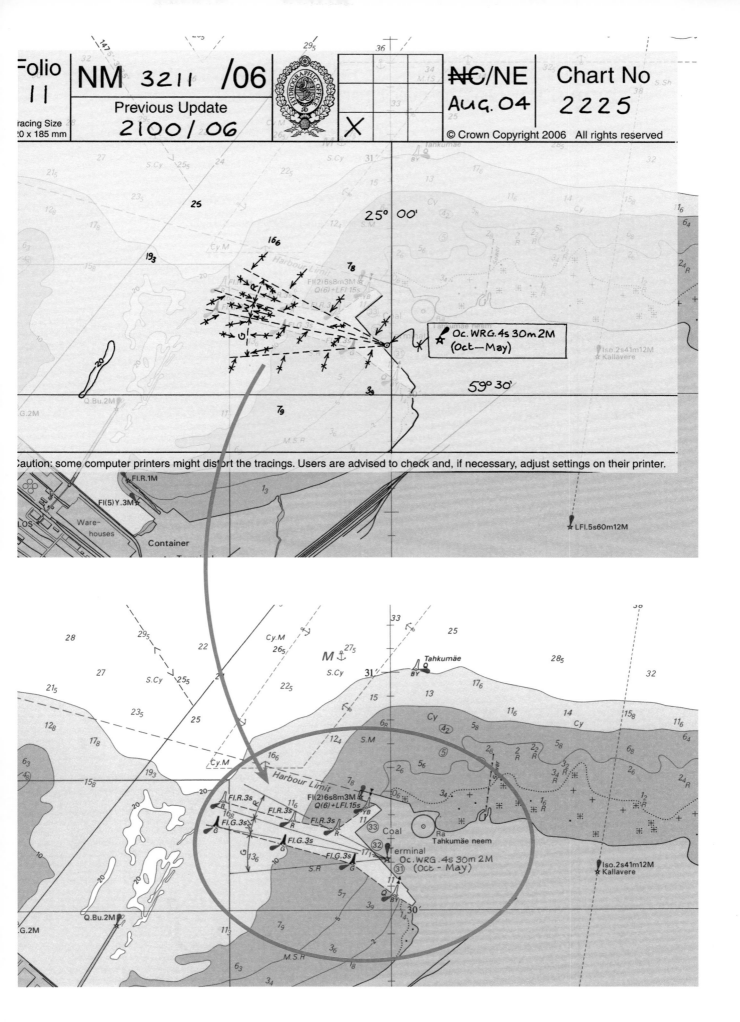

Caution: some computer printers might distort the tracings. Users are advised to check and, if necessary, adjust settings on their printer.

45

Example 10   Delete coloured light sector

667   BULGARIA - Neseburski Zaliv - Anchorage area. Light-beacon. Legend. Light.
Light List Vol. E, 2012/13, 4993, 4994
Source: Bulgarian Notices 2/42-43/12 & 2/51/12

Chart 2230 [*previous update 5907/12*] WGS84 DATUM

Insert	⚓ *Shelter*	
		42° 40′·0N., 27° 48′·9E.

Chart 2283 [*previous update 3344/12*] WGS84 DATUM

Insert	▮ Iso.R.4s2M		42° 39′·48N., 27° 43′·59E.
	circular limit of anchorage area, pecked line, radius 1·5M, centred on:	*(a)*	42° 39′·98N., 27° 48′·92E.
	legend, ⚓ *Shelter*, within:		*(a)* above
Amend	light to, Fl.G.8s2M	*(b)*	42° 39′·30N., 27° 43′·80E.
Delete	sectors at light		*(b)* above

Notes

Delete the sectors by drawing two lines across the sector lines and arcs at regular intervals. Also draw two lines through letters annotating sector colours, if shown. Charts which include coloured light flares and sectors do not depict flares at lights with sectors, when deleting all sectors at a light it is important to insert a flare at the light star, this will make the symbol more prominent.

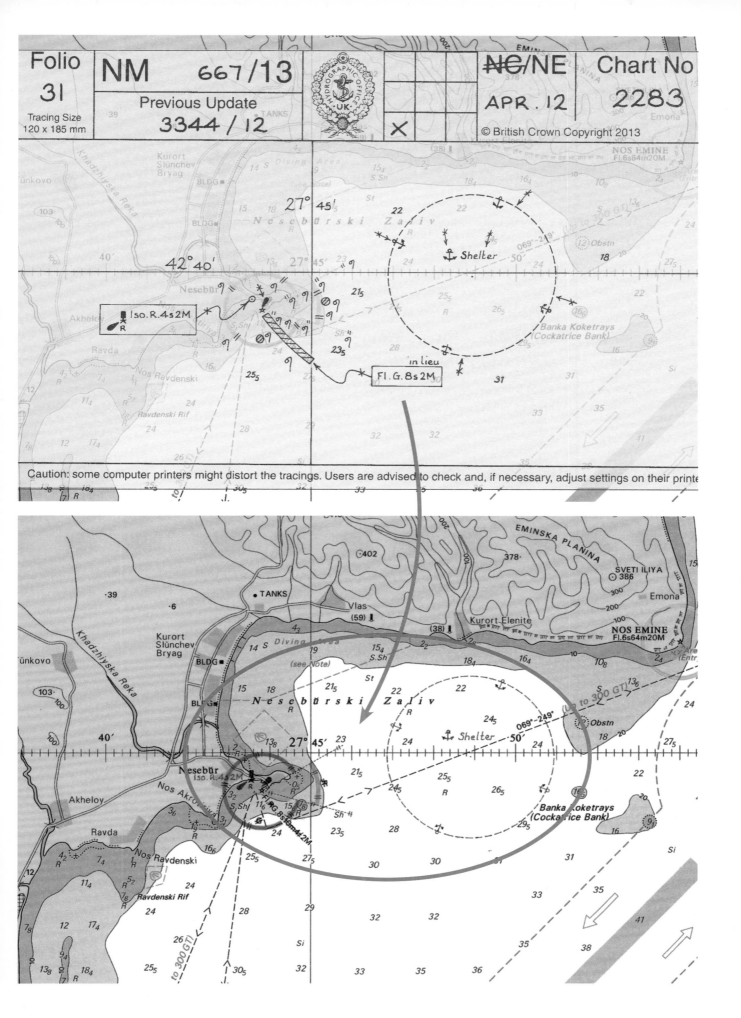

Folio 31

Tracing Size
120 x 185 mm

NM 667/13

Previous Update
3344/12

~~NC~~/NE

APR.12

Chart No
2283

© British Crown Copyright 2013

Iso.R.4s2M

in lieu

Fl.G.8s2M

Caution: some computer printers might distort the tracings. Users are advised to check and, if necessary, adjust settings on their printe

Example 11   Amend light with coloured flare

201   TURKEY - South Coast - Marmaris - Keçi Adası - Keçlada - Light.
Light List Vol. E, 2012/13, 5838
Source: Turkish Notice 48/281/12
(SEP: 2012000248878 - 1).

Chart 1054 [*previous update 5784/12*] WGS84 DATUM

Amend   light and associated flare to, Fl.2s7M   36° 47′·88N., 28° 15′·57E.

Chart 1055 [*previous update 5814/12*] WGS84 DATUM

Amend   light to, Fl.2s7M   36° 47′·88N., 28° 15′·57E.

Chart 1644 (plan C, Marmaris) [*previous update 5814/12*] WGS84 DATUM

Amend   light to, Fl.2s30m7M   36° 47′·88N., 28° 15′·57E.

Notes

A simple update similar to Example 13 - A light description has changed which includes a colour change. The update is to be applied to a chart which includes coloured light flares and sectors. In the example shown it is possible to delete part of the existing light description, other updates may require you to rewrite the complete new description, clear of existing detail, above or below the old one. Finally, insert a new flare using violet ink then delete the existing coloured flare by drawing two lines through it. This will prevent a discrepancy between the colour of the printed flare and colour stated in the light description.

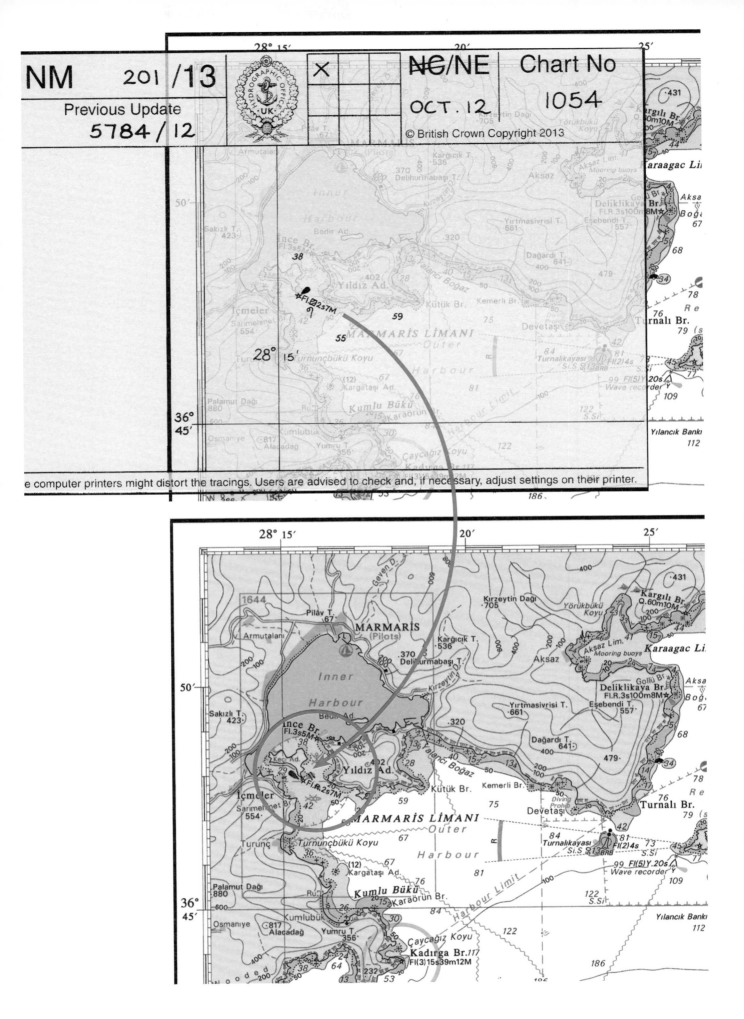

NM 201/13

Previous Update
5784/12

X

NC/NE

OCT. 12

Chart No
1054

e computer printers might distort the tracings. Users are advised to check and, if necessary, adjust settings on their printer.

Example 12   Amend the range of a light

2898   AUSTRALIA - South Australia - Approaches to Port Lincoln - Williams Island - Light.
Light List Vol. K, 2006/07, 1873
Source: Australian Notice 10/441/06
(*HH.571/009/2006-02 e26*).

Chart Aus 134 [*previous update 1357/06*] WGS84 DATUM

Amend	range of light to, 9M	35° 01´·81S., 135° 58´·21E.

Chart Aus 343 [*previous update 1124/06*] AUSTRALIAN GEODETIC DATUM

Amend	range of light to, 9M	35° 01´·8S., 135° 58´·2E.

Chart Aus 345 [*previous update 1124/06*] UNDETERMINED DATUM

Amend	light to, Fl.2·5s9M	35° 01´·7S., 135° 58´·1E.

Chart Aus 444 [*previous update 2131/06*] UNDETERMINED DATUM

Amend	range of light to, 9M	35° 01´·8S., 135° 58´·2E.

Chart Aus 776 [*previous update 2139/06*] WGS84 DATUM

Amend	range of light to, 9M	35° 01´·7S., 135° 58´·3E.

Notes

This is a straightforward change to the range of a light. The amended range should be written adjacent to the old one. Note that if space is limited, the range on its own should not be arrowed in. In these cases, it is better to write the whole description again. Make sure the 'M' is included to avoid the range being mistaken for a sounding. Remember to delete the old range by crossing it through.

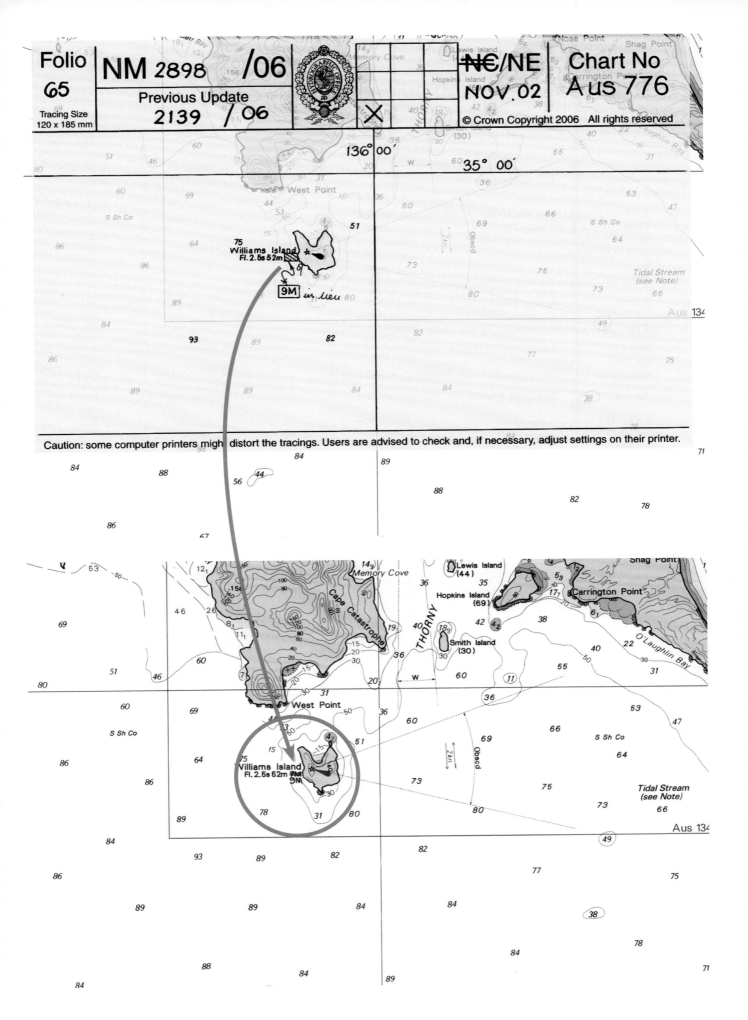

Folio
65

Tracing Size
120 x 185 mm

NM 2898 /06

Previous Update
2139 /06

NC/NE
NOV. 02

Chart No
Aus 776

© Crown Copyright 2006   All rights reserved

Caution: some computer printers might distort the tracings. Users are advised to check and, if necessary, adjust settings on their printer.

Example 13 Amend a light description

5757   PHILIPPINE ISLANDS - Mindanao - North Coast - Iligan - Light.
Light List Vol. F, 2005/06, 2268
Source: Philippine Notice 10/210/05
(*HH.552/475/-03 e14*).

Chart 3426 (plan, Iligan) [*previous update 4954/05*] UNDETERMINED DATUM

Amend   light to, Fl.G.5s37ft7M   8° 13´·93N., 124° 13´·86E.

Chart 3810 [*previous update 5592/05*] UNDETERMINED DATUM

Amend   light to, Fl.G.5s37ft7M   8° 13´·9N., 124° 13´·9E.

Chart 3811 [*previous update 4954/05*] UNDETERMINED DATUM

Amend   light to, Fl.G.5s37ft7M   8° 13´·9N., 124° 13´·9E.

Notes

This is similar to the previous example, but the whole light description has changed. Although it would be possible to change the individual elements, it is clearer to rewrite the complete new description above or below the old one. Choose an area that is clear of existing detail so that the new description can be read properly.

Refer to Example II when updating a chart which includes coloured light flares.

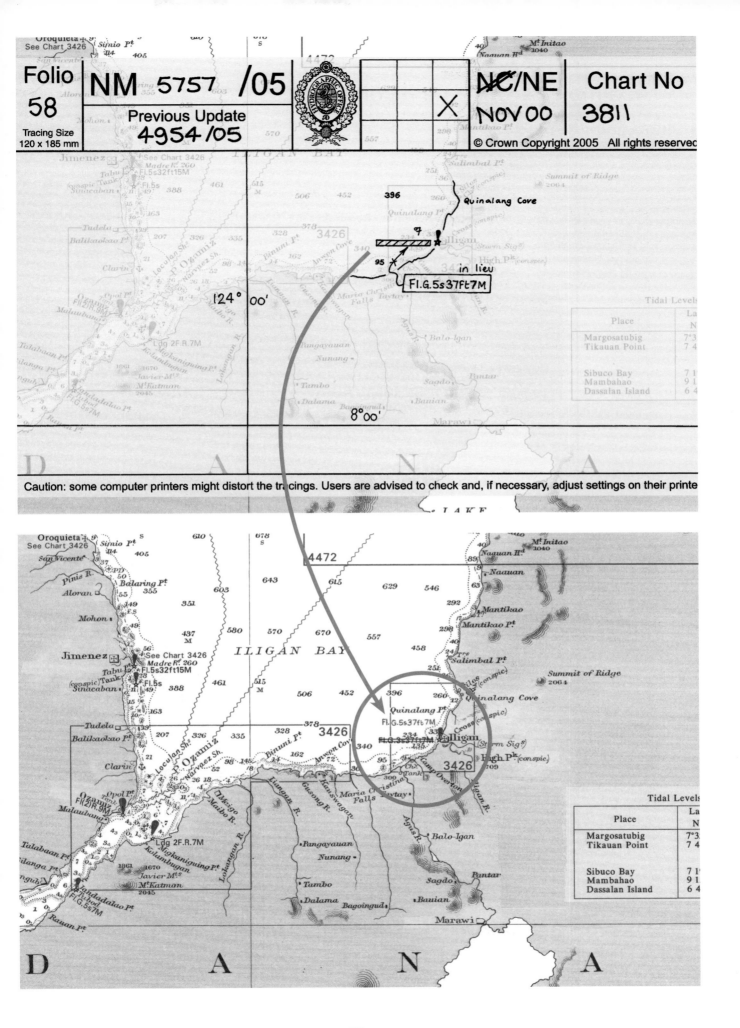

Folio 58

Tracing Size
120 x 185 mm

NM 5757 /05

Previous Update
4954 /05

N̶C̶/NE

NOV 00

Chart No
3811

Quinalang Cove

396

9

95

in lieu

Fl.G.5s37ft7M

124° 00'

8°00'

Caution: some computer printers might distort the tracings. Users are advised to check and, if necessary, adjust settings on their printe

Example 14   Insert a racon

6063   **INDIA - West Coast - Bombay Southwards - Revadanda Port - Korlai - Radar beacon.**
Light List Vol. F, 2005/06, 0558
ALRS Vol. 2, 2005/06: 78991 (50/05)
Source: Navarea VIII 671/05
(*HH.502/460/-05 e40*).

Chart 1487 [*previous update 5856/05*] INDIAN DATUM

Insert	radar beacon, Racon (O), at light	18° 32'·4N., 72° 54'·5E.

Chart 1508 [*previous update 2725/05*] INDIAN DATUM

Insert	radar beacon, Racon (O), at light	18° 32'·4N., 72° 54'·5E.

Chart 2736 [*previous update 5856/05*] UNDETERMINED DATUM

Insert	radar beacon, Racon (O), at light	18° 32'·4N., 72° 54'·5E.

Notes

This update requires a radar beacon (racon) to be added at a light. Draw a neat circle using a circle template as close as possible to the size shown on the tracing. Add the legend 'Racon (O)' alongside.

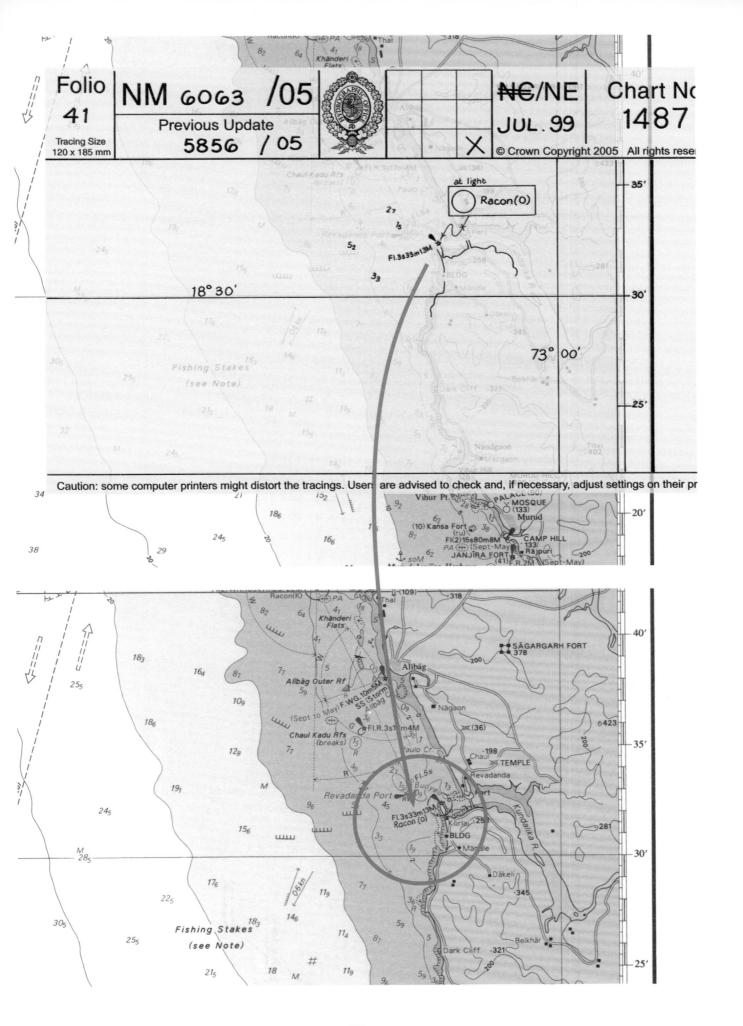

Folio 41

Tracing Size 120 x 185 mm

NM 6063 /05

Previous Update 5856 / 05

NC/NE

JUL. 99

Chart No

1487

© Crown Copyright 2005 All rights rese

Caution: some computer printers might distort the tracings. Users are advised to check and, if necessary, adjust settings on their pr

Example 15   Insert circular fish havens

2993   **SOUTH CHINA SEA - T'ai-wan - Approaches to Kao-Hsiung, Liu-Chiu Yü Westwards, Mao-pi T'ou Southwards, Kang-K'ou Wan Eastwards and Nan-jen Pi Eastwards -**
Fish havens.
Source: Taiwanese Notice 63/06
(*HH.549/210/-03 e2*).

Chart 3230 [*previous update 3608/05*] UNDETERMINED DATUM

Insert	circular limit of fish haven, dotted line, radius 900m (0·48M), depth *50*, centred on:	22° 20′·08N., 120° 14′·50E.

Chart 3232 [*previous update 1665/06*] UNDETERMINED DATUM

Insert	circular limit of fish haven, dotted line, radius 900m (0·48M), depth *50*, centred on:	22° 20′·08N., 120° 14′·50E.
		21° 48′·04N., 120° 43′·72E.

Chart 3233 [*previous update 5333/05*] UNDETERMINED DATUM

Insert	circular limit of fish haven, dotted line, radius 900m (0·48M), depth *50*, centred on:	21° 48′·04N., 120° 43′·72E.
		21° 57′·57N., 120° 54′·52E.
		22° 05′·47N., 120° 56′·80E.

Notes

This update is similar to the previous example. A circle template can be used to ensure the correct size. If a template is not available, it will be necessary to use a compass with a pen attachment to achieve the exact radius of 900m (0·48M). Place the fish symbol and the depth in open space inside the circle. Do not arrow them into position.

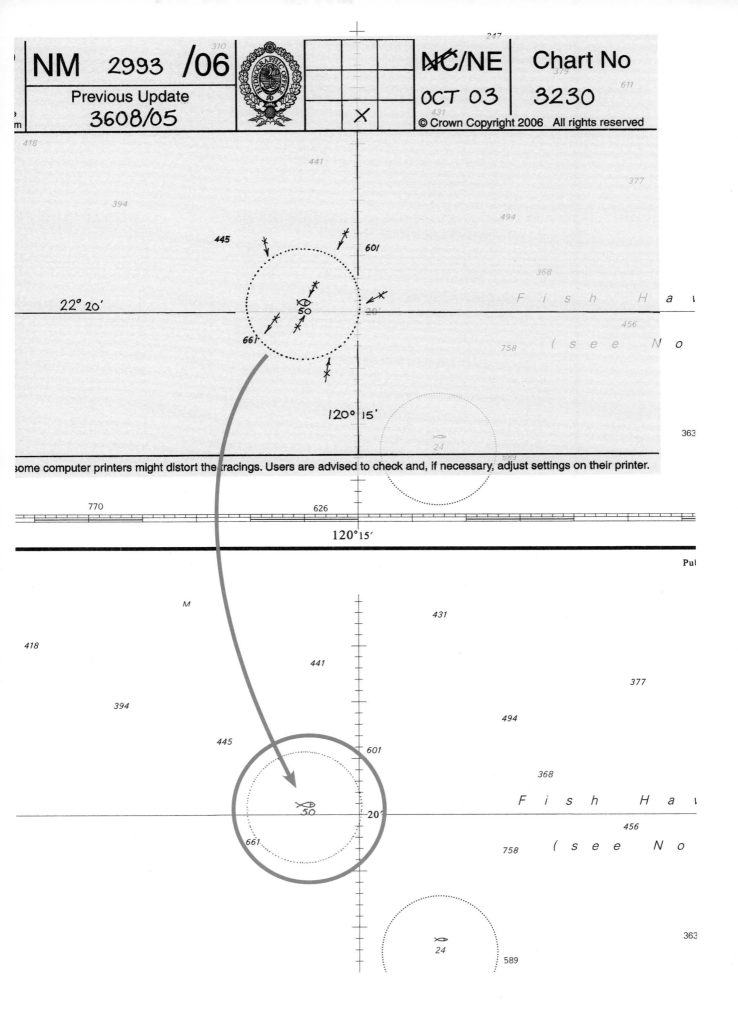

NM 2993 /06

Previous Update
3608/05

NC/NE

OCT 03

Chart No

3230

310
247
379
611
418
441
377
394
494
445
601
368
F i s h   H a
22° 20'
20'
456
661
758
(s e e   N o
120° 15'
24
363
589

some computer printers might distort the tracings. Users are advised to check and, if necessary, adjust settings on their printer.

770
626

120° 15'

Pul

M

431

418

441

377

394

494

445
601

368

F i s h   H a

20'
456

661

758
(s e e   N o

24
589

363

Example 16   Insert a submarine cable

3273   ARABIAN SEA - Pakistan - Karāchi South-westwards - Submarine cable.
Source: Pakistani Notice 19/75/06
(*HH.487/300/-02 e11*).

Chart 38 (INT 7019) [*previous update 1641/06*] WGS84 DATUM

Insert   submarine cable, 〰〰, joining:

24° 51´·45N., 66° 52´·31E. (shore)
24° 49´·48N., 66° 52´·50E.
24° 46´·37N., 66° 51´·41E.
24° 45´·22N., 66° 48´·38E.
24° 38´·95N., 66° 26´·00E.

Chart 39 [*previous update 1641/06*] WGS84 DATUM

Insert   submarine cable, 〰〰, joining:

24° 51´·45N., 66° 52´·31E. (shore)
24° 49´·48N., 66° 52´·50E.
24° 48´·52N., 66° 51´·98E.
24° 46´·37N., 66° 51´·41E.
24° 45´·22N., 66° 48´·38E.
24° 38´·95N., 66° 26´·00E.

Notes

Using the tracing or the text, mark or plot the turning points of the submarine cable on the chart. Using the hacksaw blade as a template, join up the turning points, being careful not to draw over other information on the chart. It is good practice to count the number of turning points to ensure none are missed.

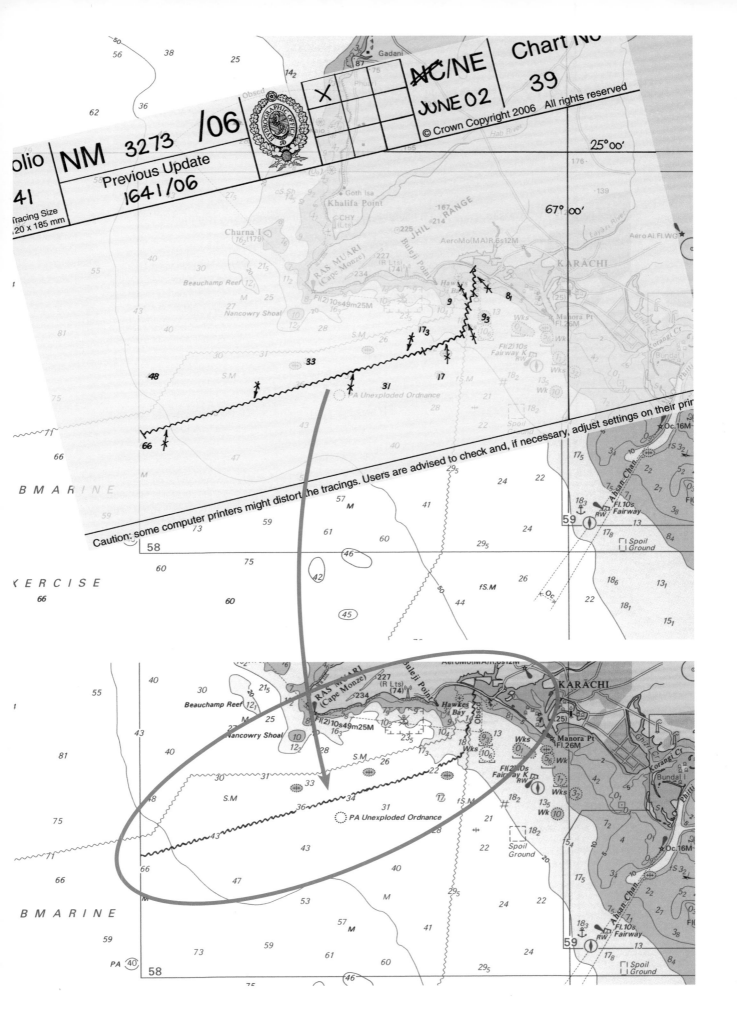

Example 17   Insert a new radio reporting line

2966   **DENMARK - Islands - Omø Island South-westwards - Radio reporting line. (continued)**

Chart 2583 [*previous update 2702/06*] WGS84 DATUM

Insert	radio reporting line, pecked line, joining:	*(a)*	55° 08´·40N., 11° 09´·00E. (shore)
			55° 05´·00N., 11° 09´·00E.
			55° 05´·00N., 11° 07´·20E.
			(W border)
	✇, direction of vessel movement 270°		55° 07´·50N., 11° 09´·00E.
	✇, direction of vessel movement 000°		55° 05´·00N., 11° 08´·20E.
	legend, *VTS (see Note)*, centred on:		55° 06´·50N., 11° 08´·80E.
Delete	radio reporting line, pecked line, joining:		*(a)* above
			55° 08´·47N., 11° 07´·20E.
			(W border)

Chart 2597 (INT 1368) [*previous update 455/06*] WGS84 DATUM

Insert	radio reporting line, pecked line, joining:	*(a)*	55° 08´·40N., 11° 09´·00E. (shore)
			55° 05´·00N., 11° 09´·00E.
			55° 05´·00N., 10° 56´·10E. (shore)
	✇, direction of vessel movement 270°		55° 06´·80N., 11° 09´·00E.
	✇, direction of vessel movement 000°		55° 05´·00N., 10° 59´·45E.
			55° 05´·00N., 11° 02´·20E.
	legend, *VTS (see Note)*, centred on:		55° 05´·20N., 11° 04´·20E.
Delete	radio reporting line, pecked line, and associated legend, *VTS (see Note)*, joining:		*(a)* above
			55° 08´·80N., 10° 57´·30E. (shore)
	✇		55° 08´·72N., 10° 59´·50E.
			55° 08´·60N., 11° 02´·85E.

Notes

This update requires a new reporting line to be drawn in. Insert the radio reporting point first in the direction stated in the text, then plot and insert the radio reporting pecked line, leaving the insertion of the legend until last.

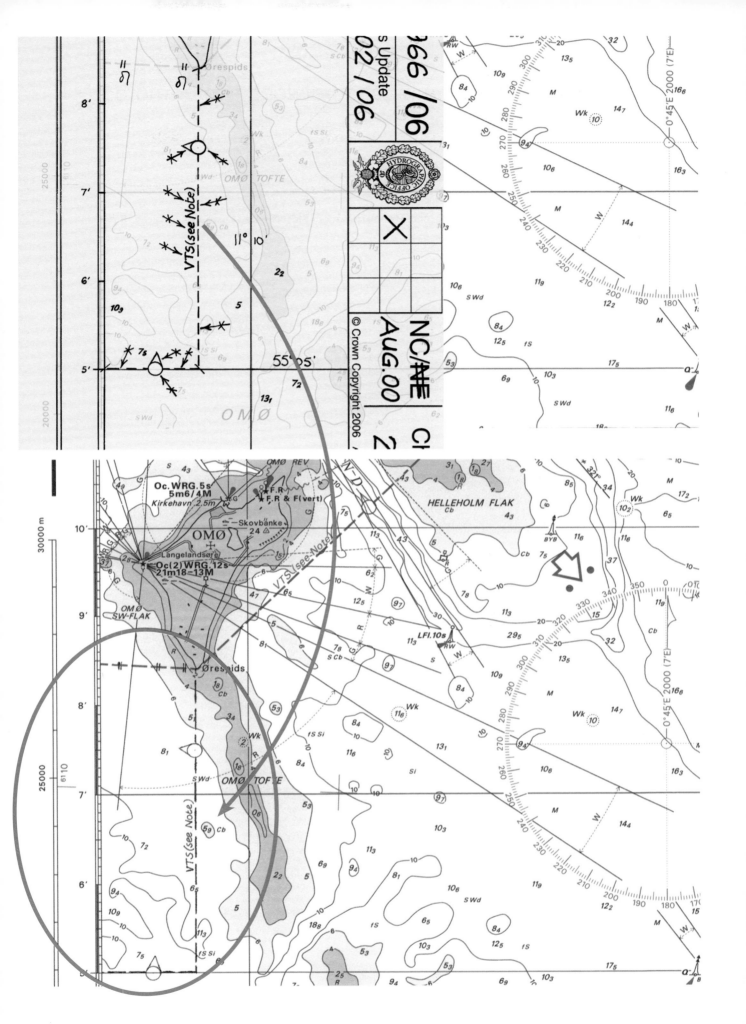

61

SECTION TWO – DIGITAL PRODUCTS

Example 18   Insert a legend between two or more positions

1966   CHINA - Yellow Sea Coast - Haiyang Dao Northwards - Shicheng Dao Eastwards - Legend. Buoy.
Source: Chinese Notices 1/1-2/07
(*HH.556/410/-04 e21*).
Note: Radar beacon remains unchanged.

Chart 1251 (plan A, Haiyang Dao to Dadong Gangqu) [*previous update 1773/07*] BEIJING 1954 DATUM		
Insert	legend, *Buoyed channel*, between:	39° 34′·8N., 122° 57′·5E.
		39° 34′·8N., 123° 00′·0E.
		39° 33′·8N., 123° 02′·5E.
		and
		39° 32′·3N., 123° 03′·5E.
		39° 29′·0N., 123° 05′·3E.
Replace	🐧 *Fl.G.4s* with 🐧 *Fl.G.4s No1*	39° 28′·7N., 123° 05′·8E.

Notes

It is common to have to insert a new legend. In most cases the legend will be centred on a particular position, but in this example the legend has to be inserted between two or more points so that it adequately covers the correct area. Plot the positions from the text or follow the instructions on the tracing. Add the new legend, spreading it between the positions. It is important to write clearly and to distinguish between capital letters and lower case. The size of the lettering should be proportionate to the size of the area the legend covers on the chart. Always position legends horizontally unless the text of the NM instructs otherwise.

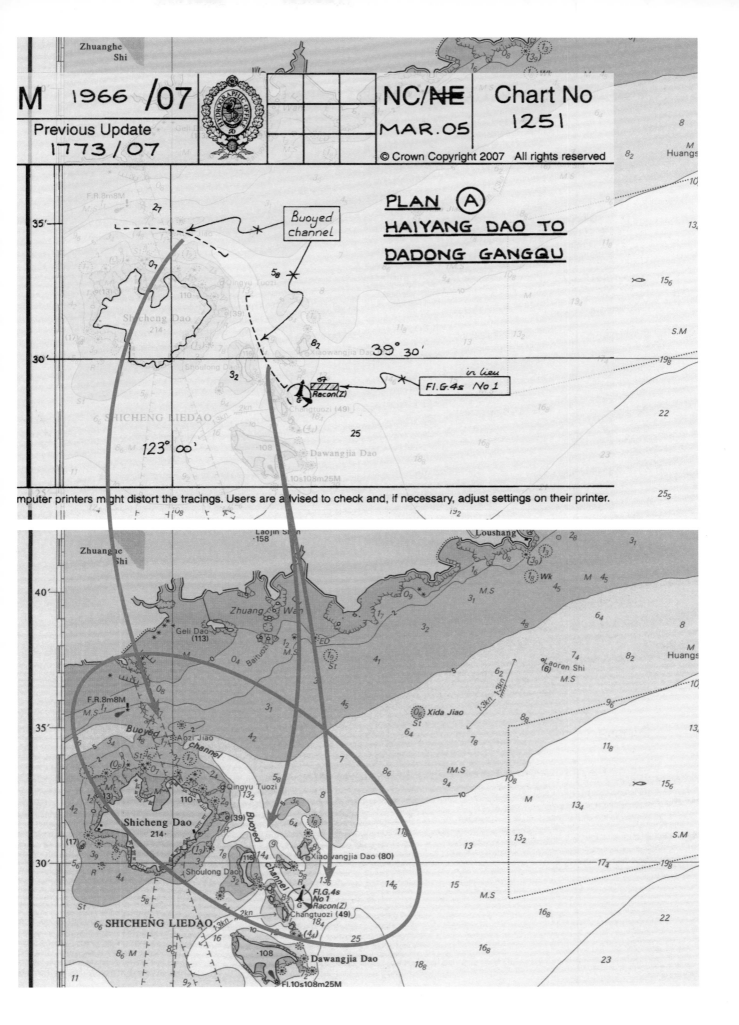

Example 19   Delete charted detail

2936   SPAIN - Mediterranean Sea Coast - Approaches to Sant Carles de la Rapita - Dredged area. Legend. Depi
Source: Spanish Chart 4851
(SEP: 2007000040704 - 1).

Chart 1515 (plan D, Sant Carles de la Rapita and Alcanar) [*previous update 2759/07*] WGS84 DATUM		
Insert	limit of dredged area, pecked line, joining:	*(a)* 40° 36´·50N., 0° 36´·25E.
		(b) 40° 35´·30N., 0° 35´·15E.
		(No 4 light-buoy)
		(c) 40° 35´·27N., 0° 35´·20E.
		(No 5 light-buoy)
		(d) 40° 36´·58N., 0° 36´·39E.
		(No 10 light-buoy)
		(e) 40° 36´·68N., 0° 36´·32E.
		(No 11 light-buoy)
		(f) 40° 36´·75N., 0° 36´·17E.
		(No 12 light-buoy)
		(g) 40° 36´·65N., 0° 36´·10E.(jetty)
	legend, *7·0m (2006)*, within:	*(a)-(g)* above
Delete	charted detail within:	*(a)-(g)* above

Notes

Insert the new feature - the limit of a dredged area. Then delete all of the charted detail within the limits, as shown on the tracing.

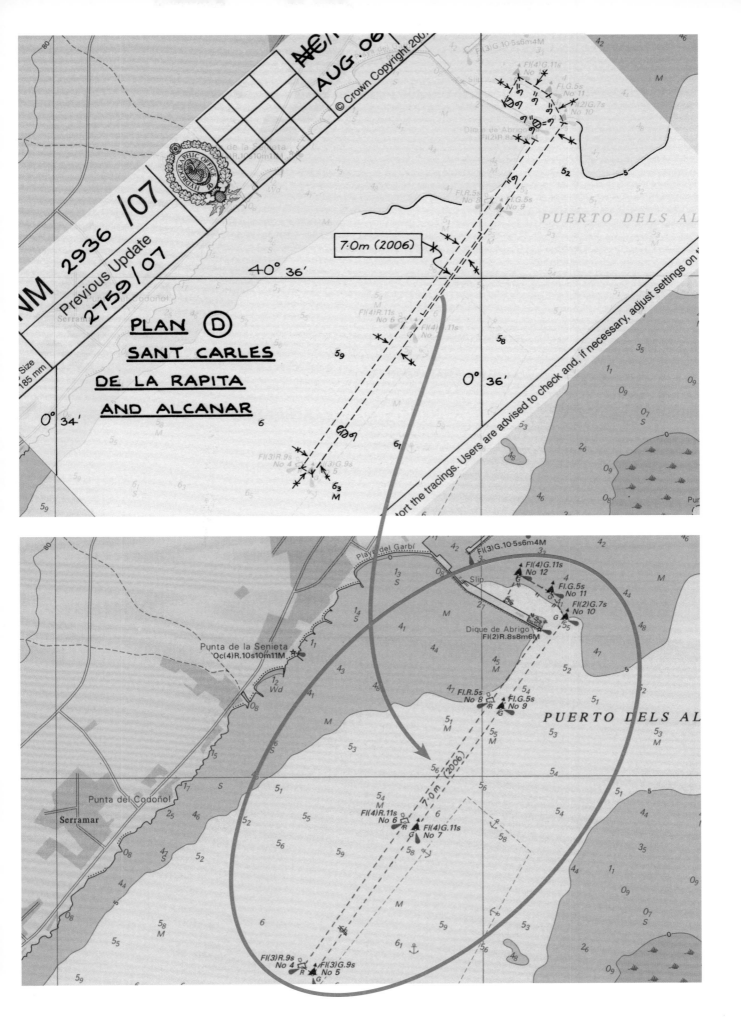

Example 20   Insert fish havens

2385   **UNITED STATES OF AMERICA - Gulf of Mexico - Louisiana - Outer Approaches to Calcasieu Pass - Trinity Shoal Southwards and Ship Shoal South-westwards - Fish havens. Platform.**
Source: US Chart 11340
(*HH.616/183/-04 e76*).

Chart 3850 [*previous update 2261/06*] NAD83 DATUM

| Insert | (15) | | 28° 00′·0N., 92° 22′·5W. |
| | | | 28° 02′·9N., 91° 31′·5W. |

Chart 3851 [*previous update 1856/06*] NAD83 DATUM

| Insert | (15) | *(a)* | 28° 02′·9N., 91° 31′·5W. |
| Delete | , adjacent to: | | *(a)* above |

Notes

A simple update which requires a fish haven and depth to be inserted in two positions. The position refers ONLY to the fish havens themselves. Draw the fish symbols in the correct positions and then add the dotted danger lines around them. The depths are added close east or west depending on the space available.

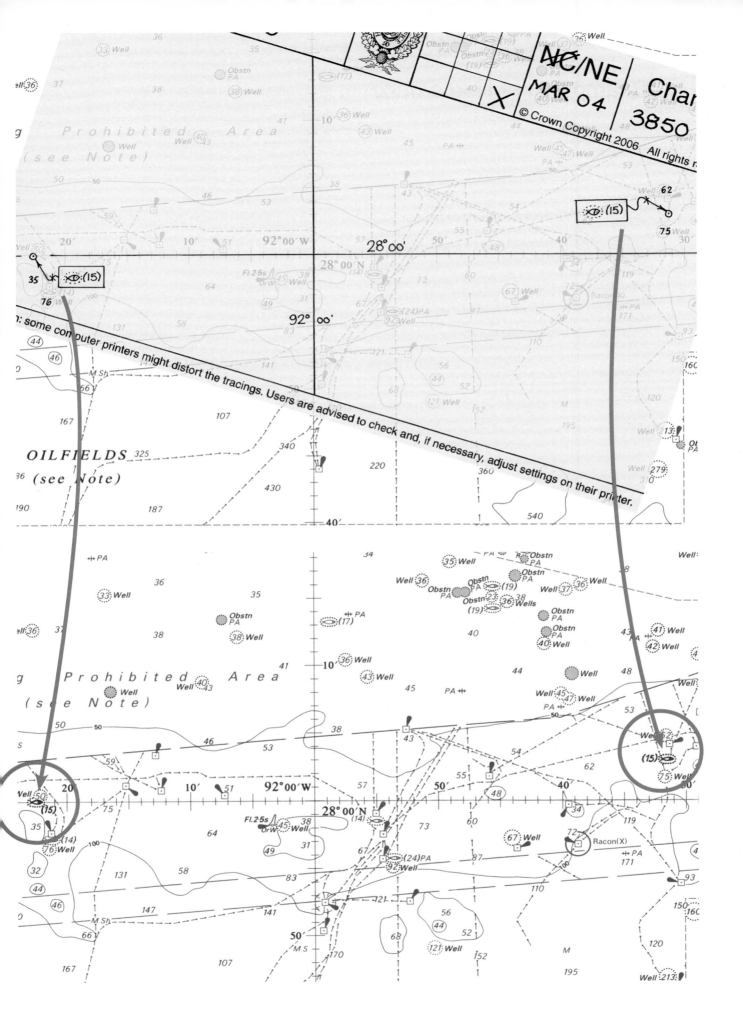

NC/NE Char

MAR 04 3850

Prohibited   Area
(see Note)

92°00'W

28°00'

28°00'N

92° 00'

n: some computer printers might distort the tracings. Users are advised to check and, if necessary, adjust settings on their printer.

OILFIELDS (see Note)

Prohibited   Area
(see Note)

92°00'W

28°00'N

Racon(X)

OILFIELDS (see Note)

Example 21   Move a buoy

2912   **UNITED STATES OF AMERICA - East Coast - Connecticut - Long Island Sound - New Haven Southwards - Buoy.**
Source: US Notice 20/12354/06
(*HH.614/475/-04 e12*).

Chart 2754 [*previous update 5163/05*] NAD83 DATUM

Move   *Fl.Y.4s 'CDA'* from: 41° 09´·00N., 72° 52´·80W.

            to: 41° 08´·68N., 72° 53´·20W.

Notes

This is the simple move of a buoy. There is no need to redraw the buoy: plot the position or mark it through the tracing. Draw a small circle at the new position and arrow the buoy to that position. Make sure the arrow does not cut through any existing detail on the chart.

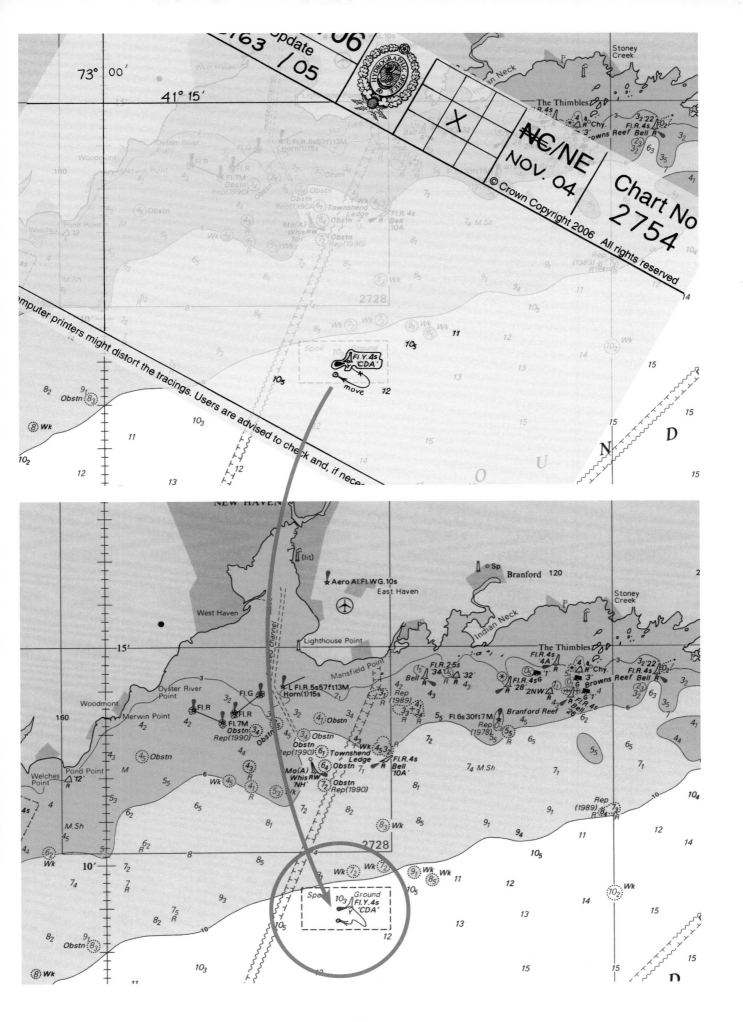

69

Example 22   Insert sounding out of position

4526   **CANADA - Saint Lawrence River - Port de Montréal - Chenal Varennes, Chenal Pointe-aux-Trembles, Longue-Pointe North-eastwards and Montréal Eastwards - Depths. Dredged depths. Dredged areas. Dolphins. Coastline.**
Source: Canadian Notice 8/1310/12
(*SEP: 2012000172164 - 1310*).

Chart 4792 (Panel A-B) [*previous update 3337/12*] NAD83 DATUM

Insert	sounding out of position 6_4	*(a)*	45° 42′ 19·1"N., 73° 26′ 18·0"W.
Replace	depth 6_8 with depth 6		45° 38′ 46·7"N., 73° 28′ 31·7"W.
Delete	sounding out of position 6_8 , adjacent to:		*(a) above*

Chart 4792 (Panel B-C) [*previous update 3337/12*] NAD83 DATUM

Insert	the accompanying block, showing amendments to dredged depths, dredged areas, dolphins and coastline, centred on:		45° 35′ 10·8"N., 73° 30′ 11·0"W.
	depth 10_7	*(a)*	45° 32′ 35·4"N., 73° 31′ 53·4"W.
Delete	depth 11_3 , adjacent to:		*(a) above*
	limit of dredged area, pecked line, joining:		45° 32′ 52·2"N., 73° 31′ 41·4"W. (shore)
		(b)	45° 32′ 50·4"N., 73° 31′ 40·2"W. (existing limit)
	dredged depth, *10,4m*, close N of:		*(b) above*

Notes

Occasionally you will be required to insert or delete a sounding 'out of position', these differ from other soundings which can be inserted in their accurate location or 'arrowed in' to avoid existing detail.

Place a dot accurately in the stated position, then write the sounding close by, draw a line between the sounding and the dot. The dot always represents the actual position.

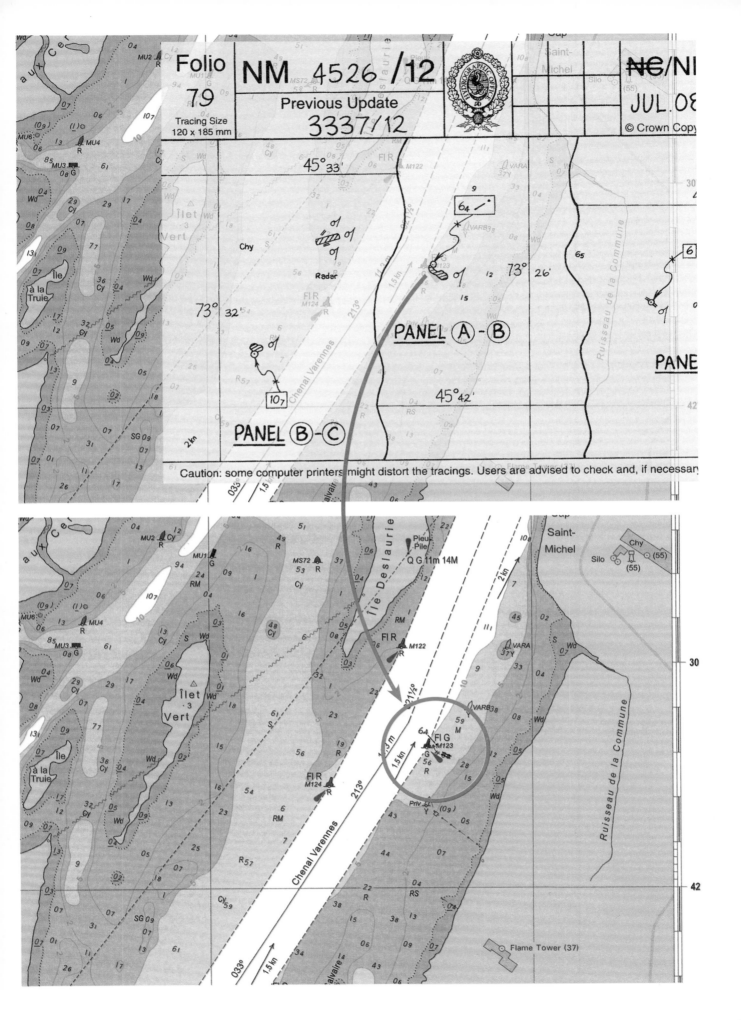

Chapter 6

How to update your Admiralty Nautical Publications

Admiralty Sailing Directions

Before using Admiralty Sailing Directions, the mariner must always:

- Check that the most recent edition of the volume is held.
- Check that all the updates in Annual Summary of Notices to Mariners Part 2 - Updates to Sailing Directions (NP247(2)) have been applied.
- Check that all updates published at Section IV of Weekly Editions of Admiralty Notices to Mariners subsequent to the publication of the most recent edition of Annual Notices to Mariners Part 2 have been applied, using the most recent quarterly check-list at Section IB of the weekly edition, and the most recent edition of Cumulative List of Admiralty Notices to Mariners.

Where it is found that the most up-to-date information is not held, the most recent editions of all Admiralty publications can be obtained from Admiralty Chart Agents, and back copies of Weekly Editions of Admiralty Notices to Mariners can also be downloaded from the UKHO website www.ukho.gov.uk.

New Editions

Sailing Directions are updated by a process of Continuous Revision, with titles republished as new editions at approximately three yearly intervals. Some volumes, indicated in the Catalogue of Admiralty Charts and Publications are on an extended cycle of approximately 5 years.

Current editions

To determine the current editions of Sailing Directions, and for information regarding the publication dates of new editions, see Annual Summary of Notices to Mariners Part 2 - Updates to Sailing Directions and Miscellaneous Admiralty Nautical Publications (NP247(2)). This information can also be found in Catalogue of Admiralty Charts and Publications (NP131), Cumulative List of Admiralty Notices to Mariners (NP234), and quarterly at Section 1B of Weekly Editions of Admiralty Notices to Mariners.

Update by Notices to Mariners

Section IV of Weekly Editions of Admiralty Notices to Mariners contains updates to Sailing Directions that cannot wait until the next new edition. These updates will normally be restricted to those deemed navigationally significant, and information required to be published as a result of changes to national legislation affecting shipping, and to port regulations. Information that is made clear by a chart updating Notice will not always be repeated in a Section IV Notice unless it requires elaboration in Sailing Directions.

Extant updates published in Section IV of Weekly Editions of Admiralty Notices to Mariners are listed in a Notice published quarterly in that Section. Those in force at the end of the year are reprinted in full in Annual Summary of Notices to Mariners Part 2 - Updates to Sailing Directions and Miscellaneous Admiralty Nautical Publications (NP247(2)).

It is recommended that updates are cut out and pasted into the parent book. Mariners may, however, prefer to keep updates in a separate file, and annotate the text of the book in the margin to indicate the existence of an update. This latter method may be more appropriate in volumes where significant numbers of updates, sometimes overlapping, may make the cut-and-paste method unwieldy and confusing. Examples are NP28 Dover Strait Pilot and NP32 China Sea Pilot Volume 3.

The record of updates page, inside the front cover of the volume of Sailing Directions being amended, should then be annotated.

Admiralty List of Lights and Fog Signals

System of updating

Each List of Lights volume is kept up-to-date in a "Continuous Revision" cycle. This means that it will be continuously revised by it's Editor(s) for a period of one year using information received in the UKHO. It will then be republished as a new edition – normally in the same month annually. Publication of a new edition is announced in Part 1 of the Weekly Edition of Admiralty Notices to Mariners.

During the life of the book important Safety of Life at Sea (SOLAS) updates are issued each week in Section V of the Weekly Edition of Admiralty Notices to Mariners. Minor updates are not issued for the paper books but are available in the Admiralty Digital List of Lights (ADLL). All minor and SOLAS updates are included in each new edition of the book.

Directions for updating

Each new edition of the Admiralty List of Lights and Fog Signals contains the latest information received by the UKHO and supersedes the previous edition. Subsequent updates to each book will be included in Section V of the Weekly Edition of Admiralty Notices to Mariners, copies of which can be obtained from authorised Admiralty Agents or via the UKHO.

The insertion of weekly updates should be recorded in the table at the front of each volume. The updates which accumulate during the book printing period will be found in Section V of the Weekly Edition of Admiralty Notices to Mariners which announces the publication of the new edition. A cut out "New Edition" note is pasted into the NEW EDITION First Updates box. New and extensively altered entries are intended to be pasted in. It is recommended that a manuscript entry is made for all shorter updates.

The entire entry for each light updated will be printed (including minor changes) and an asterisk (*) will denote which column contains an update. In the case of a new light, an asterisk (*) will appear under all columns. "Remove from list; deleted" will be used when a light is withdrawn, or a stand alone fog signal is discontinued.

The insertion of weekly updates should be recorded in the Record of Updates table below

NEW EDITION First Updates		**Vol F Edition 2011/12. NEW EDITION** Weekly Edition No. 39, Dated 29 September 2011. **NOTE:** These are the first updates issued for the New Edition.					

Week No	Date Updated	Week No	Date Updated	Week No	Date Updated	Week No	Date Updated
36/11		02/12		21/12		40/12	
37		03		22		41	
38		04		23		42	
39	29/09/11 JW	05		24		43	
40	06/10/11 JW	06		25		44	
41	13/10/11 JW	07		26		45	
42	20/10/11 JW	08		27		46	
43	27/10/11 JW	09		28		47	
44		10		29		48	
45		11		30		49	
46		12		31		50	
47		13		32		51	
48		14		33		52	
49		15		34			
50		16		35		01/13	
51		17		36		02	
52		18		37		03	
		19		38		04	
01/12		20		39		05	

Admiralty List of Radio Signals

Directions for updating

Each edition of the Admiralty List of Radio Signals contains the latest information received by the UKHO and supersedes the previous edition. Subsequent updates to each book will be included in Section VI of the Weekly Edition of Admiralty Notices to Mariners, copies of which can be obtained from authorised Admiralty Agents or via the UKHO website. Note: NP284 is only updated by new edition.

The insertion of weekly updates should be recorded in the table at the front of each volume. The updates which accumulate during the book printing period will be found in Section VI of the Weekly Edition of Admiralty Notices to Mariners which announces the publication of the new edition. A cut out "New Edition" note is pasted into the NEW EDITION First Updates box. New and extensively altered entries are intended to be pasted in. It is recommended that a manuscript entry is made for all shorter updates.

The Weekly Edition number is shown on all updates. The appropriate indexes and diagrams should also be amended if necessary. Colour versions of these may be downloaded from the UKHO website.

A cumulative list of updates is published quarterly in Section VI of the Weekly Edition of Admiralty Notices to Mariners and provides a summary list of the entries in the current editions which have been amended.

Admiralty Tide Tables

Admiralty Tide Tables are not normally amended between annual editions; however, important corrections notified after going to press will be found in Section VII of Weekly Notice to Mariners.

Catalogue of Admiralty Charts and Publications (NP131)

Each Edition of the Catalogue is correct to 30 August of the year before it is published, and the addendum (provided with it) brings it up-to-date to the date of publication for changes occurring during production. Chart users should be aware that some Flag States may require this publication to be maintained up-to-date and that some industry association audits can include this.

Users may keep the Catalogue up-to-date for new Charts and New Editions published, for charts withdrawn without replacement, and for changes to Admiralty Publications by using the information contained in:

- Section 1, and:
- the Miscellaneous Updates to Charts Notice at the beginning of Section II of the Weekly Edition of Admiralty Notices to Mariners.

Chart limits may be inserted, deleted or amended on the appropriate index sheet, and the chart numbers and title inserted or deleted on the opposite page in the appropriate place. Similar procedures should be adopted for changes to Admiralty Publications. The inclusion of updates to the catalogue should be recorded in the table provided in the Catalogue.

Mariner's Handbook (NP100)

The Mariner's Handbook is kept up-to-date in a "Continuous Revision" cycle. This means that it will be continuously revised by its Editor for a period of approximately five years using information received in the Hydrographic Office, and then republished. Publication is announced in Part 1 of Admiralty Notices to Mariners, and a listing of the current edition is updated and published quarterly in Part 1B of Admiralty Notices to Mariners and 6-monthly in the NP234 Cumulative List of Admiralty Notice to Mariners. Additionally, this list is continuously updated and available on the UKHO website at: www.ukho.gov.uk

During the life of the book, it is amended as necessary by NMs published weekly in Section VII of Admiralty Notices to Mariners. A check-list of all extant Notices, but not the text, is published quarterly in Part 1B of Admiralty Notices to Mariners. The full text of all extant Notices are published annually in January in NP247(2) Annual Summary of Admiralty Notices to Mariners – Update to Sailing Directions and Miscellaneous Admiralty Nautical Publications.

These updates will normally be restricted to those critical to the safety of navigation, and to information required to be published as a result of changes to national legislation affecting shipping, and to port regulations. It is recommended that updates issued in this way are cut out and pasted into the book. Mariners may, however, prefer to keep updates in a separate file, and annotate the text of the book in the margin to indicate the existence of an update.

SECTION TWO -

DIGITAL PRODUCTS

Chapter 7

How to obtain updates for your Admiralty Digital Publications

Updating Admiralty Digital Publications

The UK Hydrographic Office is constantly updating the information it has about Pilot Services, Vessel Traffic Services, Port Operations, Lights and Fog Signals. The Admiralty Digital Publications (ADP) product provides a mechanism by which you can obtain the latest data and update the information displayed in the applications.

Knowing When to Update Admiralty Digital Publications Data

There are several ways to check the update status of the data that ADP is using:

On the toolbar - The toolbar tells you the week number when your oldest Area was last updated. Since you can choose to update some Areas and not others, your Areas may not all be up-to-date to the same week. The toolbar will show you the week of the least up-to-date Area.

Viewing Area Properties - Right click on an Area in the filter view and select 'Properties'. The Area Properties Dialog shows the week to which each Area is updated.

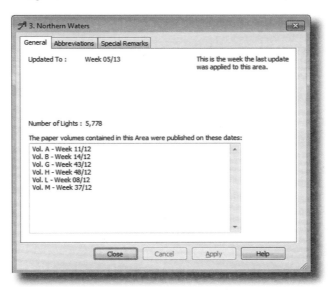

Data Updating Wizard

The updating process is managed by the Data Updating Wizard which is accessed by selecting 'Data Updating Wizard' from the 'File' menu. This wizard manages all aspects of updating your data.

The easiest and quickest way to keep your data current is to automatically update using the Internet – you will need direct access to the Internet on the PC on which you run the ADP. Alternatively you can update via email either from the PC if it has email facilities, or you can store update requests to send from a PC that does have email facilities. If you are not able to connect to the Internet or use email then you can opt to receive your update information on CD (your Agent should have asked whether you wished to receive CD Updates when you purchased ADP).

The Data Updating Wizard is automatically displayed when you start any ADP application unless you check the 'Don't automatically display the update wizard from ADLL and ADRS6' box.

Choosing an Update Path for ADP Data

You first have to choose whether you wish to get new update data from the UKHO (via direct Internet update, via an email or by manually downloading files from the UKHO website) or apply data you have already received (via an Update CD, an email or files downloaded from the UKHO website).

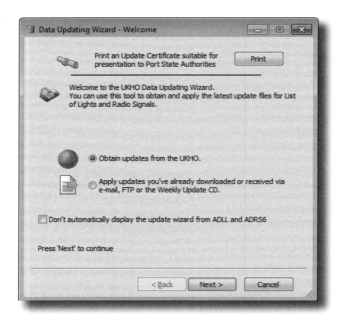

Click on the option required and choose 'Next' to continue

Choosing an Update Data Method

The data contained in the Areas can be updated in several ways:

- Update automatically over the Internet
- Request an update via email
- Connect to the UKHO website to manually download update files

The different mechanisms update your data with the same information and result in identical datasets once completed. Therefore all methods can be used to correctly and fully update your Area data.

Select the method that you wish to use and press the 'Next' button.

You can choose to update your data week by week, all methods are interchangeable and the program will understand how to apply any of the updates.

Updating Automatically over the Internet

Selecting the 'Update automatically from the Internet' option and selecting 'Next' will present you with a screen where you can choose which Areas you wish to update by checking the appropriate box.

When you want the transfer to start, click the 'Next' button and the ADP application will connect to the UK Hydrographic Office computer systems and download the information required.

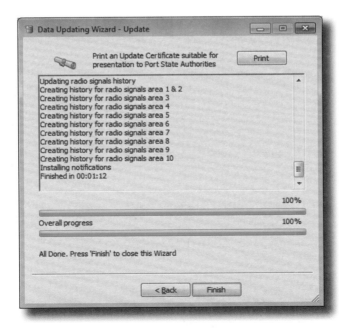

It will automatically apply the update data once downloaded. A progress bar shows you the status of the current action and a second progress bar shows the status of the overall updating operation.

During the updating operation messages are displayed in the main window showing the updates that have been applied. In addition, the Data Updating Wizard also creates a history of updates that have been applied from the last 6 updates and reports which areas have been updated. When the updating progress is complete, the 'Finish' button will be enabled which you can press to continue working with the ADP which will now be using the updated information.

Requesting an Update using Email

Obtaining an update via email is a two stage process. You must first use the Data Updating Wizard to send an email request containing information about the Areas you wish to update. This will be processed automatically at the UK Hydrographic Office and email(s) will be sent immediately with an attachment containing the data you need to update ADP. When this update is received you can use the Data Updating Wizard to import the attachment or you can simply double-click on the attachment to start the Data Updating Wizard.

If you select the 'Obtain updates from the UKHO', 'Send email to request update' option in the Data Updating Wizard you will be given the choice of Areas for which you require an update. Select one or more Areas from the list of Areas and press the 'Next' button.

You are given the option to 'Send the email now' or 'Store the request in a file to send later or to send from another PC'. If the computer that you are running ADP on has email facilities then you should choose to email the request, otherwise you should store the request in a file which you can send from a different computer.

Send the email now

If you select this option and press 'Finish', the Data Updating Wizard will create an email message automatically containing all the information needed to request your update. It is addressed to ADPUpdating@ukho.gov.uk with 'UKHOBLUR' on the subject line of the email. You just need to 'send' this email to complete your update request. The UKHO will respond with email(s) containing the update data as an attachment.

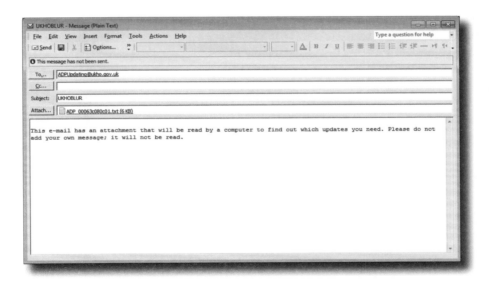

The attachment is now an .xml file:

> *Note: In order to successfully receive your updates, please make sure that:*
> *- your system allows all @ukho files to be received*
> *- the attachments are sent as .txt files*
> *- your Email system is able to accept files of up to 1MB in size*

Store the Request in a File to Send Later or to send from another PC

Selecting this option and pressing 'Next' displays the 'Data Updating Wizard - Store Update Request' screen where you can select the directory and filename to save the file to. Either type the full path and name into the text box or press the '...' button to the right of the text box to browse to a directory and enter the filename. When you click 'Finish', the required update information will be saved to the file you specified. You should send this file as an attachment to the email address specified on this page of the Data Updating Wizard and use the subject line shown.

You will receive email(s) to your update request that will contain an attachment with update data that you can import into Admiralty Digital Publications. The update data can be applied to ADP as described in the section 'Importing an Update File from an email or downloaded from the UKHO Website' shown below. If you have requested a lot of data you may receive it in more than one email, each with an attachment. You should import all the attachments. The order of importing is not important.

Connect to the UKHO Website to Manually Download Files

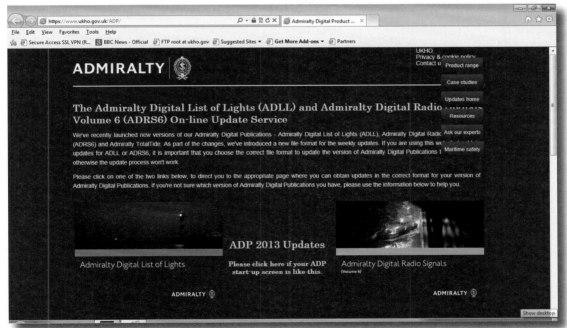

Selecting this option allows you to download the latest update from the UKHO website enabling you to update ADP. To download the correct update files for your PC, you must know the week number that your Area(s) was last updated.

Select the week number that you wish to update from but please note that if you are updating more than one Area you can only select from one update week number. For example if Area 1 is updated to week number 32 and Area 2 is updated to week number 35 you will need to perform 2 separate downloads.

Select the Area(s) you wish to update then click the 'Submit Update Request' button. Your selection will take a few moments to process. When it is complete, the updates will appear in a new window, ready for you to download. The download file can then be applied to ADP as described in section 'Importing an Update File downloaded from the UKHO Website or received in an email from another computer' shown below.

Once you have received your data you can apply the updates already received

Choosing the 'Apply Update' Data Source

The Data contained in the Areas can be updated from several data sources:

- Update from the ADP weekly Update CD
- Import an Update File from an email or downloaded from the UKHO Website

Update from a CD

When you receive your updates on CD, simply place the CD in the CD drive of your computer after selecting the 'Apply updates you've already downloaded or received' and then 'Update from CD'. The Data Updating Wizard will ask you to select the drive that the CD is located in. Either type the drive name (for example 'D:\') directly into the text box or click on the '...' button to the right of the text box and select the CD drive from the dialogue.

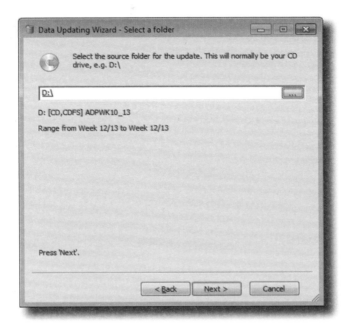

If the CD is a valid ADP Update CD then information on the Areas that are contained on the CD and the Week Number will be displayed, otherwise a message indicating that the path specified is either an 'Invalid folder' or that the CD does not contain ADP update data is displayed.

When you have selected the location from which to import the data simply click the 'Next' button. The Data Updating Wizard will say that it is ready to perform the update. Click 'Next' again and the update will commence. The Data Updating Wizard will display a screen allowing you to monitor update progress. This will update all the areas even the areas you are not licensed for.

Update from a File

87

Importing an Update File from an email or downloaded from the UKHO Website

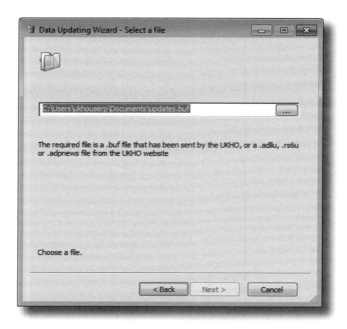

The file(s) containing the update should be saved in a directory that is accessible from the computer running ADP. Select the file by typing the path and filename into the text box or by pressing the '...' button to the right of the box and browsing to the file. When you have selected the location from which to import the data simply click the 'Next' button to import the file and the update will commence. The Data Updating Wizard will display a screen allowing you to monitor update progress.

Updates received via email can also be opened by simply double-clicking on the attachment. This will automatically start the Data Updating Wizard. If you have requested a lot of data you may receive it in more than one email, each with an attachment. You should import all the attachments; the order of importing is not important.

Chapter 8

How to install and update the Admiralty Vector Chart Service (AVCS)

This guide is designed to help you to load and maintain your AVCS data easily and quickly. It describes the basic steps necessary to use AVCS in any ECDIS. However, each ECDIS manufacturer has implemented the ENC import module differently. Users who are experienced in operating a particular model of ECDIS may require additional supporting information when managing AVCS ENCs on ECDIS equipment that they are less familiar with. For detailed installation instructions and troubleshooting information, see the AVCS User Guide and your ECDIS User Guide (supplied by the manufacturer). A copy of the AVCS User Guide is supplied with the AVCS Start-Up Pack and a digital copy can be downloaded from the UKHO website www.ukho.gov.uk/AVCS

Electronic Navigational Charts (ENCs)

AVCS is comprised entirely of Electronic Navigational Charts (ENCs) produced by Government Hydrographic Offices. It is designed to be used in conjunction with a type approved ECDIS to provide a primary navigation tool that meets the requirements of SOLAS Chapter V. ENCs contained within the Admiralty Vector Chart Service (AVCS) are produced and distributed according to well-defined international standards.

Details of the ENCs available in AVCS, including their coverage, is available in the Admiralty Digital Catalogue, which can be downloaded from www.ukho.gov.uk/catalogue, and in Admiralty e-Navigator Planning Station.

Getting Started

Your Admiralty Chart Agent will provide you with the following materials when you subscribe to AVCS for the first time:

AVCS Start-Up Pack

- AVCS Quick Start Guide;
- AVCS User Guide;
- AVCS Base Discs (a set of CDs or a DVD labelled 'Base');
- AVCS Update Disc (a CD labelled 'Update');
- Admiralty Information Overlay CD;
- Admiralty Digital Data Services End User Licence Agreement (EULA).

AVCS Licence

This may be supplied with the AVCS Start-Up Pack on hard media, e.g. floppy, CD, etc. or separately in an email. The initial licence pack will contain the following:

- A "Schedule A", (except when using Admiralty e-Navigator Planning Station) this is a PDF document listing the Folios and ENC Units that the user is licensed to use. It also lists the "Home CD" where the licensed ENCs are held. This is particularly useful as it prevents unnecessary loading of those CDs that do not contain any licensed ENCs.
- A set of ENC Permit files (PERMIT.TXT and ENC.PMT) for each ECDIS installation.
- An AVCS Certificate (a PDF document showing your vessel and licence details).

Pre-installation Checks

Data Cleansing

New AVCS users who have previously subscribed to other ENC services are strongly recommended to remove (purge) all ENC Permits and ENCs from the system before installing AVCS. There is a good reason for doing this as previously installed ENCs may become out-of-date if they are not licensed in AVCS. If the system is not purged, redundant ENCs may remain in the system database (SENC) and be available for use, even if the previous licence has expired. However unlicensed ENCs cannot be updated and the user may be unaware of this if inadvertently navigating using one. To purge the system users should consult the ECDIS User Guide supplied with the equipment.

Public Key – Is the Correct File Installed?

The ECDIS will not install ENCs from AVCS unless the correct Public Key is installed. If the correct Public Key is not installed the ECDIS will report an Authentication Failure.

Background
The ECDIS authenticates the source and integrity of encrypted ENCs from Service Providers against a pre-installed Public Key. The Public Key can be formatted in one of two ways, either an ASCII text file (.PUB) or an X509 Certificate (.CRT). Newer ECDIS (manufactured since 2003) often come with the IHO.PUB and/or IHO.CRT pre-installed as the IHO is the Scheme Administrator (SA) for the S-63 ENC Data Protection Scheme. The UKHO is a certified subscriber to this scheme. However AVCS ENCs are authenticated against the PRIMAR Public Key because many legacy ECDIS are configured to authenticate against this Public Key.

Check the Public Key
Before installing AVCS ENCs, the user must check that the correct Public Key is installed on the system. The method of managing and viewing these will vary between different makes or versions of ECDIS. If the PRIMAR Public Key is not present on the system then it will have to be installed before AVCS ENCs can be loaded. Currently the PRIMAR.CRT is held on all AVCS CDs in the root folder, most ECDIS have functionality that allows the user to import this file to the system. In these instances users should consult the ECDIS User Guide supplied with the equipment.

ECDIS Authentication Warning
The latest ECDIS, type-approved against the IMO ECDIS Performance Standards (Jan 2009), will report a warning when installing AVCS. The message reads as follows:

SSE26 - This ENC is not authenticated by the IHO acting as the Scheme Administrator

Users should acknowledge these warnings, if prompted to do so, but should not be concerned as the source and integrity of the ENCs are authenticated correctly against the PRIMAR Public Key. Other errors or warnings relating to the validity of the public key or certificate should be reported to UKHO Customer Services.

Installing and Maintaining AVCS

AVCS ENCs are currently distributed on CD-ROM and DVD media and are encrypted according to the International Hydrographic Organization (IHO) S-63 Data Protection Scheme. Initially the AVCS user is provided with ALL of the latest base and update discs which contain all the ENCs in AVCS. However these cannot be accessed by the ECDIS unless a valid set of S-63 ENC Permits are installed. Each ENC Permit is unique and is the method which gives the user selective access to particular ENCs required for the intended voyages.

Step 1: Installing AVCS ENC Permits

The AVCS ENC Permits will be supplied to you by your Admiralty Chart Agent in a zipped file. The contents of this file will depend on the user's bridge configuration as each AVCS licence allows for use on up to 5 ECDIS. When extracted, one or more sets of permit files (PERMIT.TXT and ENC. PMT) will be copied automatically into folder(s) named MASTER, BACKUP, RESERVE1, RESERVE2 and RESERVE3 depending on the number of ECDIS configured on the bridge. The contents should be extracted to a suitable media, e.g. USB flash drive or floppy disk that can be read by the system.

NOTE: The ENC Permits must be installed before any ENCs can be imported and installed on the system.

AVCS users with multiple ECDIS on board or with other systems that use ENCs (such as Chart Radar, VDR etc) should be very careful to load the correct permits for the intended system. Each system may require its own unique set of permits. Failure to do so will result in an error being reported similar to the following:

- CRC failure permit could not be read
- Failure to uncompress ENC data file
- Decryption failed

Step 2: Installing AVCS ENCs

AVCS data is delivered on a series of CD-ROMs (or a single DVD) labelled Base and a CD-ROM labelled Update. Each Base disc contains all the ENC base cell files and associated updates for those producer nations identified on the CD label. Users are provided with all ENCs in the service but can only access those ENCs that they are licensed for. The AVCS Base discs are periodically re-issued to free up space on the AVCS Update CD, this is currently about every 8 weeks. The AVCS Base discs must be loaded first before the AVCS Update CD can be loaded.

The AVCS Base disc label contains the date and week of issue. Users should be careful to only load an AVCS Update CD that is newer than the installed bases. The status of the latest AVCS Base CDs is published in the weekly Admiralty Notices to Mariners bulletin. Users with internet access can check the status of the latest AVCS Base CDs using the following link:

http://www.ukho.gov.uk/AVCS

Click on the Licensing and Updating tab to view the AVCS distribution and issue dates.

There are currently 9 AVCS Base CDs but this number may grow as more ENCs become available for distribution within AVCS. It is unlikely that users will need to install all of the CDs in order to load all licensed ENCs. Users should refer to the Schedule A or Admiralty e-Navigator Planning Station to avoid the unnecessary loading of some CDs. A small sample of the information contained in the Schedule A is provided below:

RFA03 – English Channel		Holding Expiry Date 31.12.2010	
Cell	Title	Home CD	AVCS Update
GB301820	Isles of Scilly and Western Approaches	AVCS Base 3	N/A
GB301840	Land's End to Falmouth	AVCS Base 3	AVCS Update
GB302020	Falmouth to Looe	AVCS Base 3	N/A

PACAS Asian Seas		Holding Expiry Date 31.12.2010	
Cell	Title	Home CD	AVCS Update
GB202868	Tokongkemudi to Natuna Utara	AVCS Base 9	N/A
GB202870	Pulau-Pulau Leman to Badas	AVCS Base 9	AVCS Update
GB202872	Selat Karimata and Approaches	AVCS Update	N/A

Users should be aware that, depending on the manufacturer, each type of ECDIS manages the import of ENCs in one of two ways:

1. The ECDIS loads the ENC base data (base cell) in the first instance and then the user has to update as a separate operation;
2. The ECDIS will manage the import of ENC base data and all updates in a single operation.

Users should consult the ECDIS User Guide supplied with the equipment to confirm which operation is appropriate to the system.

The appropriate base discs must be installed in the system and licensed ENCs imported according to the instruction provided in the ECDIS User Guide. The process must be repeated until all licensed ENCs are imported to the system.

Step 3: Installing AVCS ENC Updates

AVCS is updated on a weekly basis and updates are distributed via your Admiralty Chart Agent on CD-ROM. The only exception to this is in a week when the AVCS Base Discs are re-issued; in these instances an AVCS Update CD will not be issued. The AVCS Update CD contains all new ENCs, new editions of ENCs and ENC updates issued since the last set of AVCS Base discs were issued. The CD is cumulative so the user only has to load the latest week number. Users can update their system using the AVCS Update CD or remotely over the internet using the Admiralty Updating Service or Admiralty e-Navigator Planning Station.

NOTE: Although ECDIS equipment and ENCs are designed to be very reliable, there is a slightly increased risk of problems occurring when ENCs are being added, removed or updated. For this reason, you must not attempt to make changes to the installed AVCS ENCs when the equipment is being used for primary navigation or if the vessel is committed to an imminent departure.

Step 4: Maintaining AVCS ENC Holdings

Your Admiralty Chart Agent will provide you with a weekly Update CD, when it is practical to do so. The AVCS Base discs are re-issued about every 8 weeks depending on the amount of data on the Update CD. It is important that users do not attempt to load an Update CD that is not consistent with the Base discs. For example, you should not attempt to load an update that is older than the Base discs held on board and installed on the ECDIS.

Note: When new AVCS Base discs are re-issued the user MUST install these before attempting to load the latest AVCS Update CD.

Periodically the user will be supplied with an updated set of AVCS ENC Permits. New permits are issued for any ENC that has had more than one new edition. The reason for this is that older ECDIS will only install ENCs with the same edition number as contained in the permit.

An AVCS permit file is specific to a particular week as described in the Schedule A. It is important that users do not install these unless they have the corresponding Update CD for the same week. Failure to follow this advice when using an ECDIS type-approved before 1 January 2009 could render some of the installed ENC unavailable for use in the ECDIS. The only exception to this rule is if additional coverage is required in case of emergency or a change to a planned route.

AVCS ENC updates are also available over the Internet using the Admiralty Updating Service or Admiralty e-Navigator Planning Station.

Emergency AVCS ENC Permits

Under certain circumstances it may be necessary for a vessel to gain access to an unlicensed AVCS ENC at very short notice. For instance if the vessel has to divert from a planned route due to a medical or safety related emergency. In these emergency situations only, individual AVCS ENC Permits can be obtained from the UKHO 24 hours a day, 365 days a year. These permits can be transmitted direct to the vessel by email, by fax, or simply by reading the AVCS permit string(s) out over the telephone or radio. This service is also available for the ECDIS and ARCS services.

To obtain an AVCS emergency chart permit please contact UKHO Customer Services, quoting your name and contact details, the vessel name, the User Permit Number of your ECDIS system and the ENC(s) required.

Chapter 9

Admiralty Information Overlay

What is the Admiralty Information Overlay?

The Admiralty Information Overlay contains additional information which is considered navigationally significant and can be used in conjunction with ENCs to improve safety of navigation when using ECDIS.

The Overlay contains information about changes or hazards of a temporary nature, such as changes to aids to navigation, advance notice of permanent changes, new survey information which will later be issued as an ENC update, and additional information of relevance to mariners which is not currently included in national ENCs. The Overlay includes all Admiralty T&P NMs in force worldwide and additional information from the comparison of ENCs and Admiralty paper charts, published as ENC Preliminary NMs (EP NMs).

The UKHO can only include information in the Overlay where it exists in the UKHO archive of hydrographic information. AVCS includes ENCs produced by national Hydrographic Offices that are the equivalent to their local paper chart series. Where there is no equivalent Admiralty paper chart, the UKHO does not have any additional information and the Overlay shows a 'No Overlay' feature. Additional information, such as local T&P NMs, may be available in these areas from other sources. When navigating in these areas, mariners should ensure that all appropriate sources of information have been consulted.

Installing the Admiralty Information Overlay

Compatible Equipment

The Overlay can be displayed on compatible ECDIS equipment and also in Admiralty e-Navigator Planning Station. Please see the UKHO website at www.ukho.gov.uk/AVCS for an up-to-date list of compatible equipment, or consult your ECDIS supplier. Most ECDIS equipment installed prior to 2010 will require an upgrade before it will be able to display the Overlay.

Admiralty e-Navigator Planning Station allows the Overlay to be displayed against all ENCs on your AVCS licence. To allow your licensed ENCs to be installed on e-Navigator, please ask your Admiralty Chart Agent to include the e-Navigator *User Permit* on your AVCS licence. You will then be issued with a permit file for e-Navigator that allows all licensed ENCs and the Overlay to be installed.

Installing Overlay Permits

The Overlay data is protected in the same way as ENCs and requires a permit to unlock the data. This permit will automatically be added to all Chart Permit files used with e-Navigator. Please notify your Admiralty Chart Agent if you wish to use the Overlay on any other compatible ECDIS so that the Overlay permit can be added to the Chart Permit files for that equipment.

The Overlay permit will be loaded at the same time as all ENC permits when the Chart Permit files are loaded (see Loading Charts for the First Time above).

Installing Overlay Data

The Overlay data is provided on a single CD that contains both base data and all updates up to the date of issue. Therefore only the latest CD is required for installation and all others can be discarded.

The Overlay data is loaded in to the display equipment (e-Navigator or ECDIS) in the same way as ENC data (see Loading Charts for the First Time). Note that some ECDIS may require you to run an 'Update ENC' process after loading the base data to ensure that all updates on the disk are also applied.

Updating the Overlay

Updates to the Overlay are issued weekly on CD, along with the weekly AVCS Update CD, and are also available over the Internet through e-Navigator. Updates on CD should be loaded in the same way as loading ENC updates (see Maintaining the Chart Outfit above).

The data volume in each weekly update is normally small. However it is necessary to issue a New Edition of the Overlay every 6 months, which consolidates all update data into a base data set that may be over a hundred megabytes in size. It is impractical for most users to download this volume of data over the Internet and an Admiralty Information Overlay CD should be used.

Updating the Overlay in Planning Station

AVCS customers can also request the weekly Admiralty Information Overlay (AIO) update when downloading AVCS updates using the 'Get Update' function. For a full explanation of this method of updating please see page 111 in Chapter 11

> When an Overlay new edition is issued (see above), the new edition must be installed before any further updates can be applied. For users who normally update over the Internet this means that an Overlay update CD will need to be installed before further Internet updates can be applied.

Using the Admiralty Information Overlay

Displaying the Overlay

The Overlay is designed to be displayed on top of a standard ECDIS chart display and can be switched on and off without changing the underlying chart.

Only those features relevant to the chart in use are displayed. As the user zooms in or out, the ECDIS will automatically select charts of a relevant scale and the Overlay features relevant to the selected charts will be displayed. For example, a Temporary NM that applies only to a large scale chart will not be displayed when smaller scale charts of the same area are being used.

T&P NMs

All Admiralty T&P NMs that are in force are included in the Overlay. Each NM is displayed as a simple red polygon (usually rectangular) with red hatched fill which indicates the area affected by the NM. Each NM carries the same NM number that is used in the Admiralty Notices to Mariners Bulletin.

The full text of the NM is included as an associated text file which can be displayed by selecting the 'Temporary Notice to Mariners' or 'Preliminary Notice to Mariners' feature in the ECDIS Pick Report. Any associated diagrams can also be viewed through the Pick Report.

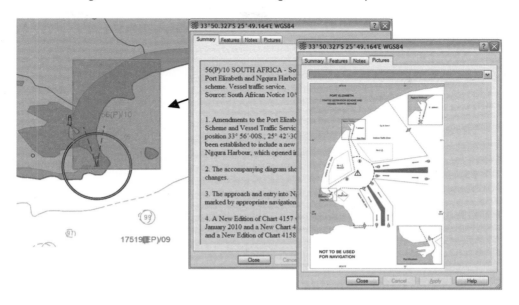

Figure 1 Preliminary (P) NM showing text and diagram

EP NMs

ENC P (EP) NMs contain additional information that is specific to ENCs and cannot be published as a standard Admiralty T&P NM. These NMs are displayed in the same way as T&P NMs, as a simple red polygon (usually rectangular) with red hatched fill which indicates the area affected by the NM. Each NM is allocated a unique EP NM number.

The full text of the NM can be viewed in the ECDIS Pick Report against the Information attribute. Where additional information is needed to explain the NM an associated picture file displays an image showing the ENC superimposed over the current paper chart information.

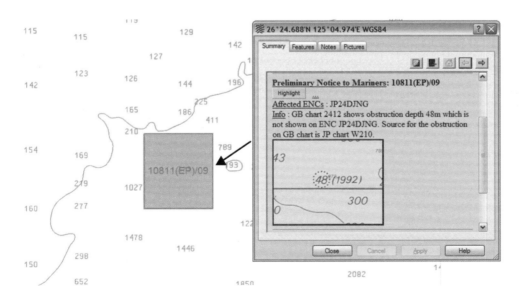

Figure 2 ENC P (EP) NM

LIVERPOOL JOHN MOORES UNIVERSITY
LEARNING SERVICES

'No Overlay' Feature

Where there is no equivalent Admiralty paper chart, the UKHO does not have any additional information and the Overlay shows a 'No Overlay' feature. This feature is displayed as a grey polygon with a grey hatched fill indicating the area where there is no overlay information.

Additional information, such as local T&P NMs, may be available in these areas from other sources. When navigating in these areas, mariners should ensure that all appropriate sources of information have been consulted.

Using the Overlay to Navigate

The Admiralty Information Overlay contains additional safety and NM information which is considered navigationally significant and may affect your voyage. This information should be referred to when planning your passage and may also be temporarily displayed during route monitoring.

When planning your passage it is normal to review all charts (and therefore ENCs) that are expected to be used on the passage. When these charts are reviewed the Overlay should be turned on and any features that could affect the planned route should be investigated. Those features that are significant for the planned passage should be marked using Mariner's Navigational Objects, which can be displayed by the ECDIS when navigating. Sufficient information should be attached to the Mariner's Navigational Objects to inform the navigator of the action to be taken when they are encountered on passage.

If the ECDIS is capable of displaying the Overlay, Overlay information may temporarily be displayed when navigating. To avoid clutter on the ECDIS display the Overlay should normally be turned off and should only be turned on for brief periods when required for reference. Therefore Mariner's Navigational Objects should be used to draw attention to relevant Overlay features when the Overlay is turned off.

Chapter 10

Admiralty Raster Chart Service (ARCS)

Introduction

ARCS charts are high quality, digital facsimile copies of British Admiralty (BA) paper charts, and share a common numbering system. Chart availability is published in the 'Catalogue of Admiralty Charts and Publications' (NP131), in the Admiralty Digital Catalogue which can be downloaded from the UKHO website at www.ukho.gov.uk/catalogue, and in Admiralty e-Navigator Planning Station.

Additional charts are announced in Admiralty Notices to Mariners. ARCS charts provide a world-wide electronic chart coverage that can be used within Electronic Chart Display and Information Systems (ECDIS).

This guide is designed to help you gain maximum benefit from using the service, and should be used in conjunction with your ECDIS User Manual.

Service Overview

Over 3200 ARCS charts are now available on 11 Raster Chart (RC) CD-ROMs, covering the world's major trading routes and ports. Each CD-ROM contains an average of 270 charts, but as many as 350 can be stored. Regionally based Chart CD-ROMs RC1 to RC10 contain standard BA nautical charts, while RC11 contains ocean charts at scales of 1:3,500,000 and smaller. However, please note that some ocean charts are provided on regional Chart CD-ROMs to provide continuous coverage, instead of RC11.

New Editions and New Charts

New Editions and New Charts for ARCS and BA paper charts are issued simultaneously. They are supplied on each weekly Update CD-ROM until incorporated into their respective 'Home' CD-ROMs at the next issue. Please note that New Editions and New Charts replacing charts already licensed, are supplied free of charge until the licence expiry, but will require loading from the Update CD-ROM (in instances where one chart is replaced by more than one new chart, access to all replacement charts is provided).

Occasionally, it is necessary to issue new charts in advance of their intended date of validity, for example a change in regulations commencing on a future date. In such cases the current chart will co-exist with the new chart until the date of implementation, the earlier chart being indicated with a suffix 'X'. The system will allow access to both charts for the period of overlap by the issue of new chart permits. At the date of implementation, the old ('X') edition should be deleted from the system.

Licence Period

ARCS is licensed for a period of 12 months. At the start of the licence period users will receive an ARCS Start-Up Pack containing all 11 Raster Chart CD-ROMs, the latest Update CD, a Chart Permit file and a Schedule A from their Admiralty Chart Agent. The Chart Permit file unlocks the charts added to the licence and the Schedule A lists the licensed charts for your records.

During the licence period, ARCS Update CDs will be supplied weekly to enable the licensed charts to be maintained for Notices to Mariners. You will also be provided with all New Editions and replacement charts within your licence. These updates are also available by email and over the internet using the Admiralty Updating Service or Admiralty e-Navigator Planning Station.

When your ARCS licence expires you will no longer be able to load ARCS Update CDs. Unless the licence is renewed the charts will not be updated for Notices to Mariners and will therefore not meet SOLAS chart carriage requirements. Licence renewal can be arranged by your chosen Admiralty Chart Agent.

Data Verification

ARCS charts are supplied with the same guarantee of accuracy and reliability as BA paper charts, and are subject to stringent checks to ensure that the raster image is identical to the paper one. Data quality is likely to be more reliable on newer surveys at larger scales, and the source data diagram can be used to assess the quality of source data. This is typically ten times smaller than the chart to which it refers, and should be interpreted with care at the limits of specific survey areas. Occasionally, plotting on the source data diagram will not be possible because it cannot be referenced to the main chart with sufficient accuracy.

ARCS CDs are protected by encryption to ensure data integrity and to allow licensing of charts. Access to ARCS charts is provided by the Chart Permit files supplied; these will have been generated for, and will only work on, the ECDIS for which they were ordered. They will be provided on disc or emailed to you.

ARCS Start-Up Pack

This pack should include:

- ARCS User-guide
- Packaging (to hold your CDs, Chart Permit files, etc)
- 11 ARCS RC CD-ROMs (these contain all available ARCS Charts)
- 1 Update CD
- Admiralty Digital Data Services End User Licence Agreement (EULA)
- Chart Permit files (supplied by your Agent on floppy disc or via email)
- A 'Schedule A' which lists all ARCS charts incorporated in the licence (except when using Admiralty e-Navigator Planning Station).

If any of these items are missing from your Start-Up pack, please contact your Admiralty Chart Agent.

Getting Started

Loading Charts

The procedure for loading ARCS charts varies from ECDIS to ECDIS however the same general principles apply and these are outlined below. You should consult your ECDIS system manual for detailed instructions.

Chart Permits

Access to the charts on the ARCS RC CD-ROMs is provided by Chart Permit files. These are supplied by your Agent and consist of 2 files; Gb.lcn and Gb.ncp. The Chart Permit file contains permits for all the licensed charts.

Loading ARCS for the First Time

Chart Permits - insert the Permits supplied into the ECDIS by following the procedures supplied by the manufacturer.

Loading Base Charts - insert the ARCS RC CD-ROM(s) for the relevant chart permits held (refer to the Schedule A supplied or to the ARCS RC CD-ROM diagram in the section below). Most ECDIS will allow you to choose whether to load all licensed charts or just those of your choice; some may prompt you to load specific RC or 'Area' CDs. Once the charts have been installed you should update your charts by loading the latest ARCS weekly Update CD.

Loading Latest ARCS Update CDs - the Admiralty Raster Chart Service Update CDs contain cumulative information. If you receive more than one ARCS weekly Update CD at the same time, you only need to load the most recent one. Having installed the ARCS RC CD-ROM(s) and loaded the latest ARCS weekly Update CD, the ECDIS system will then display the latest ARCS information available.

Maintaining the Chart Outfit

Update CDs

ARCS Update CDs are issued weekly containing all the latest 'Notice to Mariner' corrections, New Editions and any New Charts issued. Updates for ARCS charts are provided in line with Admiralty Notices to Mariners; New Editions and New Charts are issued in the same week as for paper charts.

On receipt of the Update CD you should load the new data using the update procedure specified in your ECDIS manual. The process should be automatic, but as required by the ECDIS specifications you will be asked by the ECDIS to accept the updates. Again, if you receive more than one weekly Update CD at the same time, you only need to use the most recent because they are cumulative.

It is possible that your ECDIS will occasionally report warnings or errors during the update process. Whilst it is not possible to be definitive in this matter, users are advised that a warning can be accepted as being very unlikely to corrupt data already loaded, but an error should be treated more seriously and the chart should only be used with caution since it may not reflect the latest Notices to Mariners information. Users should notify UKHO Customer Services if their ECDIS system reports errors on loading of charts or updates.

> Note:
> If replacement ARCS RC CD-ROMs have been issued containing New Editions of certain charts, subsequent updates for those charts cannot be applied until the New Edition has been installed.

NB: Stored Routes and Updates

Updates applied to the ECDIS may affect previously stored routes. It is important to check the effect of any updates on a stored route prior to its use.

Re-Issued ARCS RC CD-ROMs

The UKHO periodically re-issues new ARCS RC CD-ROMs in order to integrate newly available Base data that is temporarily held on the Update CDs. ARCS RC CD-ROMs will be accompanied by an ARCS weekly Update CD as normal.

On receipt of re-issued ARCS RC CD-ROMs it is necessary to reload all required ARCS charts from the CD.

New Chart Permits

You will automatically be issued with all necessary Chart Permits to provide access to newly available or replaced charts within your licence. Please ensure that you load new Chart Permits when you receive them to ensure your ECDIS has the capability to use the latest charts from the latest CDs.

Schedule A

The Schedule A lists the content of all the charts that have been licensed. Updates to this will be provided with the weekly Update CDs where this is necessary. The update will list details of cancelled and replaced charts.

Licence Expiry

Once the licence period for the service has ended, the ECDIS system will prevent the loading of further updates until the licence is renewed. Access to ARCS charts will cease 30 days after expiry of the licence. The expiry date is shown on the Schedule A and on the Chart Permit file.

> Note:
>
> ARCS must be kept up-to-date for Notices to Mariners to meet IMO SOLAS requirements. An ECDIS using charts beyond the expiry date of the licence will not meet chart carriage requirements.

Adding Chart Coverage

Additional charts may be obtained during the licence period through your chosen Admiralty Chart Agent who will supply new Chart Permits to 'unlock' the newly added charts.

Licence Renewal

Approximately four weeks before licence expiry you should receive a renewal reminder from your Admiralty Chart Agent. The ECDIS will display an intermittent warning one month before expiry and a permanent warning following expiry. To ensure continuity of service, please confirm requests for renewal at least two weeks in advance of the expiry date.

Service Details

Features of ARCS

Produced by the UKHO for the commercial shipping industry, ARCS charts meet the International Hydrographic Organisation's (IHO) S-61 Raster Navigational Chart (RNC) standard. They may, with Flag state approval, be used in ECDIS (in conjunction with an appropriate folio of up-to-date paper charts) to meet chart carriage requirements for areas where ENCs are not yet available. See IMO ECDIS Performance Standard (1.9 as amended).

Each ARCS Chart shares the same numbering as the BA paper chart from which it is produced.

Please note that certain charts included on an RC CD-ROM may not currently be available for use, pending approval from the national hydrographic offices concerned.

Chart Coverage

ARCS charts available in the Admiralty Raster Chart Service are available on 11 'RC CD-ROMs' for the geographic areas covered by each RC CD - see Figure 3 below.

Please note that ARCS RC11 covers the whole area shown in the diagram as it contains ocean charts at scales of 1:3,500,000 and smaller.

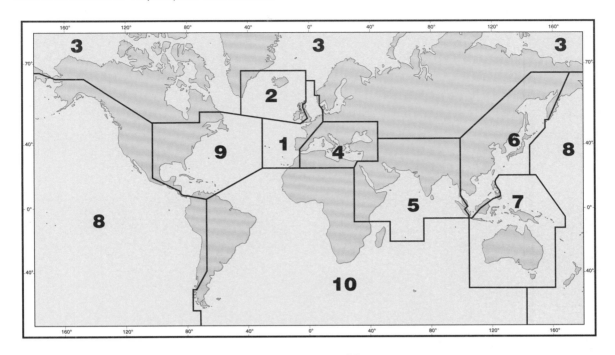

Figure 3 ARCS regional CD coverage

T&P Notices to Mariners (NMs)

A complete listing of Admiralty T&P NMs are included on the ARCS Update CD. This is in text file format and can be printed out. Some ECDIS systems have a capability to display the appropriate T&P NMs to the user.

Chapter 11

How to update Admiralty products using e-Navigator

Admiralty e-Navigator Planning Station

Admiralty e-Navigator Planning Station is a software application for use by the navigating team on board vessel. The application comprises of three key functions:

- **Holdings Management System** – Mariners can track the status of all Admiralty digital and paper charts and publications in a single place, giving them quick and easy visibility of the status of products held on board. Missing data for digital charts can be downloaded almost instantaneously through Planning Station, ensuring the vessel remains safe and compliant. The Holdings Management system also integrates with paper chart updating services supplied by our partners to offer complete management of paper charts and publications.

- **Admiralty catalogue** – The integrated Admiralty Catalogue allows the mariner to identify and purchase the best combination of charts and publications needed to navigate a plotted route safely, compliantly and cost effectively. Orders placed from Planning Station are sent direct to your Admiralty distributor, allowing you to purchase Admiralty products when you need them.

- **Product Viewer** – An integrated chart viewer enables viewing of subscribed digital chart datasets such as the Admiralty Raster Chart Service (ARCS), Admiralty Vector Chart Service (AVCS) and the Admiralty Information Overlay (AIO). Customers of Admiralty Total Tide, IHS Fairplay and DNV Navigator can also view these products through Planning Station.

Planning Station Communications

Admiralty e-Navigator Planning Station requires either a broadband internet connection or email access to download data or to place orders. Below are the communication methods which can be used with Planning Station:

- **Connected Email** – Planning Station is attached to a defined email address. Data downloads and product orders created are automatically sent from that email account. Planning Station will then pick up and import the returned data or new permits from the email account inbox.

- **Removable Drive** – Attachments are created when a data download or order is placed. The request file is attached to an email which is sent to a specific email address. The UKHO servers will send data back to the email address used to send the request file. New permits will be sent when the product order has been approved by your Admiralty distributor.

- **Internet (Https)** – Requests placed from Planning Station are sent through the internet. Catalogue and digital chart updates are downloaded in a single connection. New chart permits for orders approved by your Admiralty distributor can be retrieved by requesting a Catalogue update (Check My Status).

To view or change your selected Planning Station communication method;
go to User Settings > Communication Method and select from Email, Removable Drive or HTTPs
(Internet). The default option is Removable Drive.

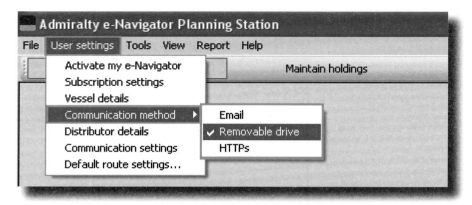

How to keep Planning Station Catalogues up-to-date

When the Admiralty e-Navigator Planning Station software is activated it downloads the latest catalogue files. It is important that the Planning Station catalogues are updated regularly as these contain Notice to Mariner and Edition details as well as the latest Admiralty product catalogue. Planning Station compares the products held on board against the catalogues, highlighting charts and publications which require updating.

New catalogue files are released every Thursday and can either be received with the Weekly Update email or requested from the Home Page via 'Check My Status'.

Catalogue updates are requested from the Home screen by selecting 'Check My Status' in the bottom right corner. This is also used to check that the latest catalogues are held in Planning Station.

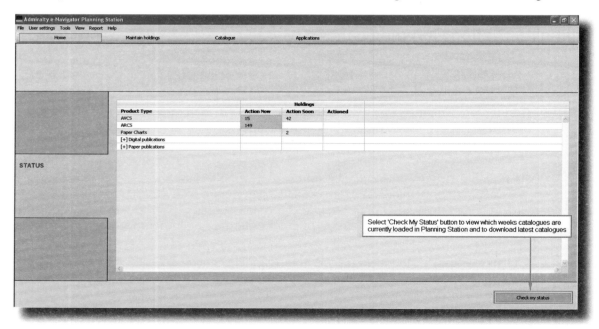

When 'Check My Status' is selected the Catalogue Update window opens, listing the current Planning Station catalogues held. Select the 'OK' button to download the latest catalogues available or select 'Cancel' to close the window.

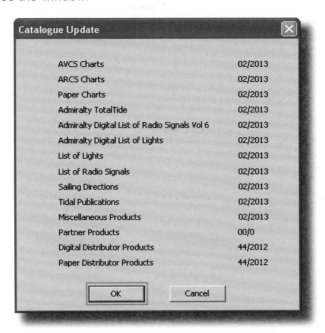

The catalogues will be downloaded using your preferred communication method; Removable Drive, Connected Email or Internet (HTTPs). For basic details see the previous section 'Planning Station Communications' or refer to the Planning Station User Guide for comprehensive guidance.

How to keep paper products up-to-date using Planning Station

A master, or 'holdings', record of the vessel's paper charts and publications held can be maintained in Planning Station. This record is passed back to the shore-based users of Admiralty e-Navigator Fleet Manager, meaning that it can be viewed by Shipping Company and Distributor users.

The integrated catalogues within Planning Station mean that it can also be used to view and manage the status of paper charts and publications held on board. This enables the bridge team to manually add and remove paper products to reflect the true holdings. The update status of the paper products held can be manually managed so that mariners know if they are up-to-date.

When a new paper chart or publication is received on board it should be manually added to the Planning Station Holdings. To do this go to the Catalogue screen, select the paper product needed from the Product Selection Filers and then Search for the new chart or publication using the geographical display or list catalogue.

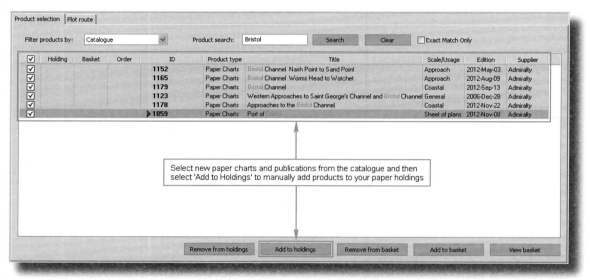

When the new paper products have been selected, use the 'Add to Holdings' button to manually add selected paper products to your holdings. Paper products which are no longer held on board can be manually removed using the 'Remove from Holdings' button.

After adding the new paper products to your holdings, go to the Maintain Holdings area and select the product type added from the Product Selection Filter. The holdings added will now be displayed on the geographical display and in the holdings list. Use the Search tool to find and select all paper holdings that have just been manually added; these will all appear in yellow colouring with the 'Update Status' as 'Not Installed'.

Right-click over the 'Week' column and select 'Current Edition' to confirm that it is the latest edition of the chart or publication that has been received on board.

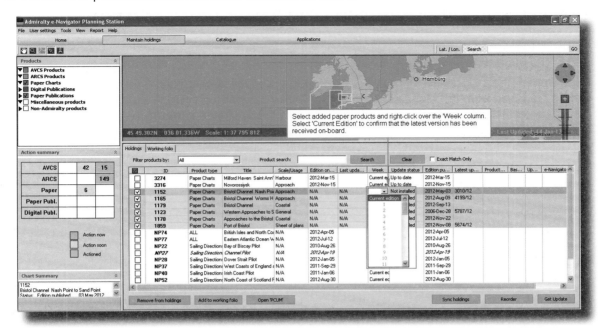

All of the new products received on board will now have 'Current Edition' as the 'Week'. Right-click on the 'Week' column again but this time select the Notice to Mariner week number that the products are currently updated to.

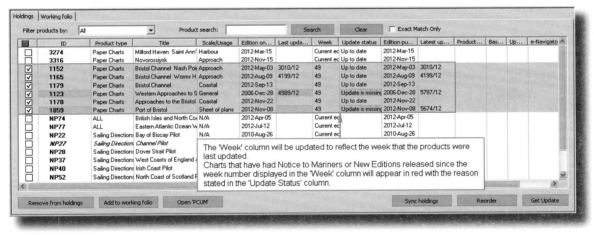

The 'Week' column will be updated to reflect the Notice to Mariner week number that the products were last updated. Any charts which have had a Notice to Mariner correction or a New Edition published since that week will be coloured in red with the reason stated in the 'Update Status' column.

The 'Week' column should be updated using the above process every time a New Edition is received or a Notice to Mariner update is applied.

Using a Paper Chart Updating Module in Planning Station

Paper products can also be managed using third party software applications which may be available from your Admiralty Distributor. These applications support paper chart updating by downloading the Notice to Mariners text and block corrections. Some paper chart updating applications can also link with Planning Station to provide a single integrated solution for keeping all paper products updated.

If the Paper Chart Updating Module (PCUM) used on board is compatible with Planning Station it can be launched from the Maintain Holdings screen by selecting the 'Open PCUM' button, providing the PCUM is installed on the same PC as Planning Station. The master record for your paper chart holdings will now be maintained using the Paper Chart Updating Module and will be synchronised with Planning Station as changes are applied to the PCUM.

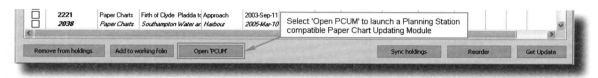

How to keep digital charts up-to-date using Planning Station

Admiralty e-Navigator Planning Station provides a useful tool for vessels to manage and maintain the digital charts held on board. The Maintain Holdings area provides mariners with visibility of digital charts held with the integrated catalogues highlighting any charts that need updating. Urgent updates required for a voyage can be downloaded using the vessels communication method of choice (See section Planning Station Communications).

Data can be downloaded for digital charts displayed in the Maintain Holdings area in red or yellow colouring. These will show with an update status of 'Update is Missing' (Red), 'New Edition is Available' (Red) or 'Not Installed' (Yellow). Download the missing data by selecting the required charts from the holdings list and then selecting 'Get Update'.

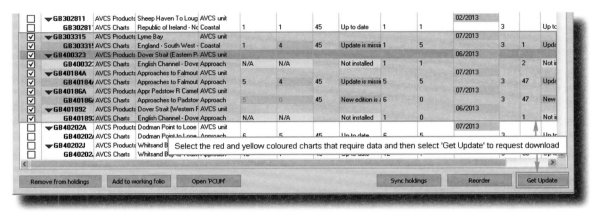

The 'Get Update' window will open listing all updates that have been requested. Select 'Submit Order' to download chart updates for the digital charts that are listed.

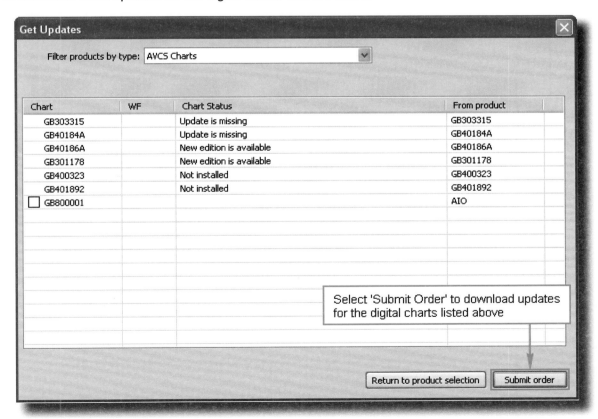

If you are downloading AVCS Updates and would also like to download Admiralty Information Overlay updates, see section 'Updating the Admiralty Information Overlay in Planning Station' for details.

The 'Get Update' request to download digital chart data will now be processed and sent back to you. How the data is received depends on your selected Planning Station communication method. See section **Fulfilment of Digital Chart Updates** for details.

Updating the Admiralty Information Overlay in Planning Station

AVCS customers can also request the weekly Admiralty Information Overlay (AIO) update when downloading AVCS updates using the 'Get Update' function.

To do this, select any urgent AVCS updates that are needed from the Maintain Holdings tab. The 'Get Updates' window will open listing the AVCS products that updates were requested for. The AIO is displayed as GB800001 which will appear by default at the bottom of the list of AVCS products. Select the GB800001 tick box to request the latest AIO updates.

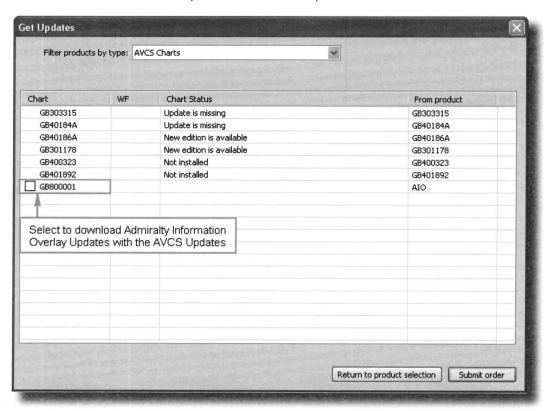

An 'Order AIO Updates' window will open. This contains a warning message that the AIO updates contain images and, although the UKHO has made data volumes as small as possible, this may mean that in some weeks a large amount of data could be downloaded. AIO updates can also be applied via the weekly AIO Update CD.

To continue downloading AIO Updates; fill in details of the latest AIO Edition and Update held on your ECDIS and/or Planning Station and then select 'Yes'. Select 'No' to cancel the AIO update request.

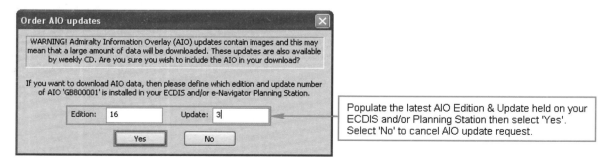

Note: If you have not previously applied AIO data to your ECDIS and/or Planning Station, it is recommended that you first load this from an AIO data CD due to the large file size. If internet download sizes are not an issue, the whole AIO can be downloaded by populating the Edition and Update boxes with the number '0' (Zero). This will download a full set of AIO data.

The AIO Edition and Update that you populated will now appear on the 'Get Updates' window, next to the GB800001 box. This indicates that you will download all AIO updates that have been issued since the specified Edition/Update. Select 'Submit Order' to download the AVCS and AIO Updates.

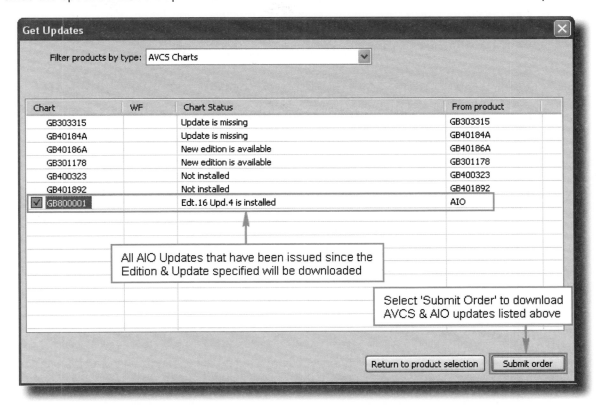

The 'Get Update' request to download digital chart data will now be processed and sent back to you. How the data is received depends on your selected Planning Station communication method. See section **Fulfilment of Digital Chart Updates** for details.

Fulfilment of Digital Chart Updates

The method used to receive digital chart data on Planning Station following a 'Get Update' download request depends on which communication method has been selected. Below are details of how 'Get Update' download requests are fulfilled using each of the Planning Station Communication Methods:

- **HTTPs:** When a 'Get Update' is submitted using HTTPs, the requested data will be downloaded directly from the UKHO servers on demand. The data will be sent directly back to Planning Station and a wizard shall open to guide you through the process of exporting an exchange set file to be applied to ECDIS.

- **Direct Email:** The direct email method connects your Planning Station application to a specified email account of your choice. When a 'Get Update' is submitted, Planning Station will send a data request from your email account to the UKHO server. An email will be sent back to your Inbox containing a data file. Planning Station will check the email Inbox for the response email at time intervals specified in your settings (Default to check every 10 minutes). When Planning Station checks your Inbox it will find the response email and import the attached data file. This will open a wizard to guide you through the process of exporting an exchange set file to be applied to ECDIS.

- **Removable Drive:** When a 'Get Update' is submitted using the Removable Drive method, Planning Station creates a request file which needs to be attached to an email sent to the UKHO servers. An email is sent back with a data file attached that needs to be manually imported into Planning Station (Tools>Apply Update). If your Planning Station and communications PC are separate, you will need to use either a Removable USB Drive or CD to transfer the request and data files between the computers. When the data file has been imported into Planning Station, a wizard will open to guide you through the process of exporting an exchange set file to be applied to ECDIS.

Updating the ECDIS

It is important that your latest permits are applied to each ECDIS on board. When the Weekly Update email is imported or a 'Check My Status' request is completed, the latest permits available are applied to Planning Station. Your AVCS or ARCS permits and downloaded data can be exported at any time by going to Tools>ECDIS updates/permits.

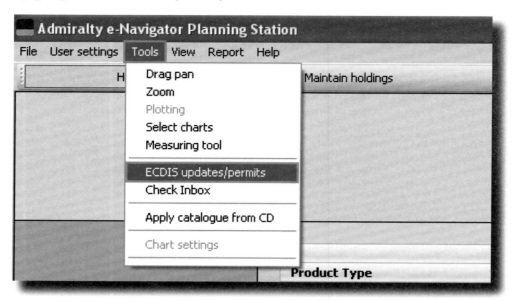

The 'ECDIS updates/permits' wizard will open; you can either select to export only your latest permits or you can export your permits and all data that was downloaded during a 'Get Update' request.

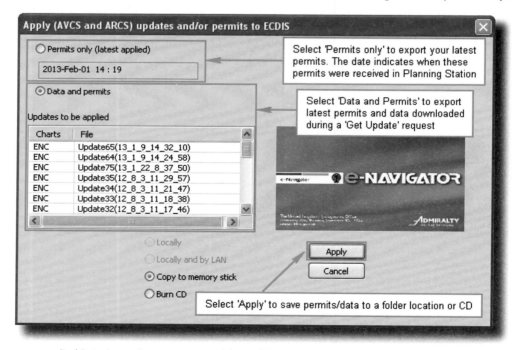

When your permits/data have been exported from Planning Station, the permit file and/or exchange set need to be applied to every ECDIS on board.

The above 'ECDIS updates/permits' wizard will appear automatically when a 'Get Update' response is received in Planning Station to guide you through exporting the downloaded data to apply to ECDIS.

Updating your ECDIS Status in Planning Station

When data has been loaded to your ECDIS it is important that you synchronise Planning Station to display the updated ECDIS status. You will need to synchronise Planning Station with your ECDIS when any of the following processes have been applied:

- Data loaded to ECDIS from UKHO Base/Update CD
- Data downloaded from Planning Station (via 'Get Update' process) is applied to ECDIS
- Data received with the Weekly Update Email is applied to ECDIS

To synchronise the status of your Planning Station and ECDIS you will need to use the 'Sync Holdings' wizard. This is opened using the 'Sync Holdings' button in the bottom right corner of the Maintain Holdings page.

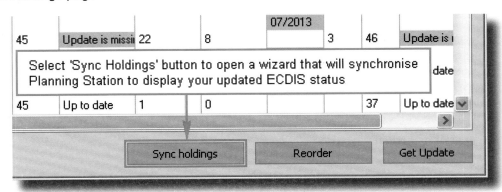

The synchronise holdings wizard will open giving you three options.

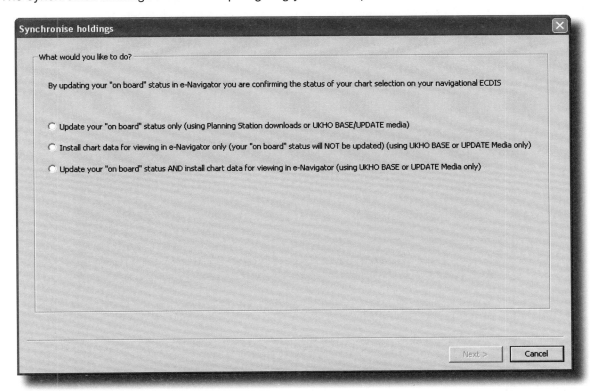

Below are details of when each wizard option should be used:

- **Update your "on board" status only (using Planning Station downloads of UKHO BASE/UPDATE media)** - This option should be used when you have downloaded digital chart updates from Planning Station using the 'Get Updates' function. All download data must first be applied to ECDIS; followed by selecting this option in the Planning Station synchronise holdings wizard. Selecting this option will update the 'on board' column on the Maintain Holdings page. This option can also be used when you have applied UKHO Base/ Update data to your ECDIS; it will update your Maintain Holdings 'on board' column but will not load data into Planning Station.

- **Install chart data for viewing in e-Navigator only (your "on board" status will NOT be updated) (using UKHO BASE or UPDATE Media only)** - This option should be selected if Planning Station is used only for viewing digital chart data, and you want to load data from a UKHO Base or Update CD. This option should only be selected if the ECDIS status is not being updated.

- **Update your "on board" status AND install chart data for viewing in e-Navigator (using UKHO Base or UPDATE Media only)** - This option should be selected when a UKHO Base/Update CD has already been applied to ECDIS and you now want to update your Planning Station record and load chart data. This will update your Maintain Holdings 'on board' status to show that the data CD has been applied to ECDIS and load chart data for viewing in Planning Station.

Select the required option and then go to 'Next' to continue through the synchronise holdings wizard.

Managing your Working Folio

Within Planning Station you can create and edit a subset of your holdings, called a Working Folio. This allows you to identify and manage only those digital and paper products that are relevant to your current voyage or area of operation.

You can also receive update and new chart data for digital charts that are in your working folio included with the Weekly Update Email. See section **Receiving Data with the Weekly Update** for details.

The Working Folio tab is located on the Maintain Holdings page:

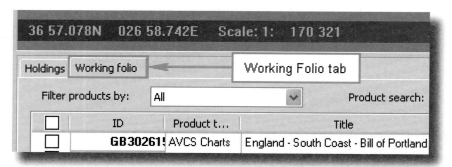

To add items to your working folio; go to Maintain Holdings and select the Holdings tab. Search for and select the required products and then click on 'Add to working folio' at the bottom of the page.

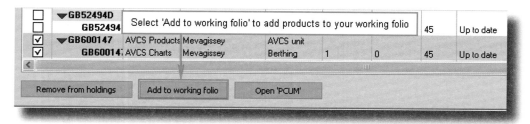

To remove items from your working folio; go to the Working Folio tab, select the products you want to remove and then click on the 'Remove from working folio' button.

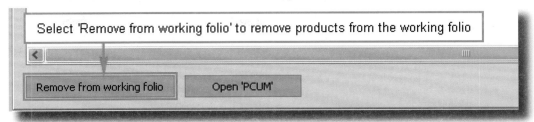

Updating Other Admiralty Products in Planning Station

If your Admiralty Digital Publications and Admiralty Paper Publications are out-of-date and new editions are available, these can be ordered from your Admiralty Chart Agent via Planning Station using the Catalogue screen.

For more information on ordering products in Planning Station or for more information about the e-Navigator service please contact your Admiralty distributor.

Applying the Weekly Update Email

The Weekly Update Email is sent to AVCS and ARCS customers that have chart permits which have changed during the previous week (E.g. Permits have been cancelled, replaced, added or withdrawn). The Weekly Update Email is sent out by the UKHO every Thursday and contains the updated AVCS or ARCS permits which need to be applied to ECDIS.

Planning Station customers receive the Weekly Update Email with an e-Navigator specific file attached (.ads).

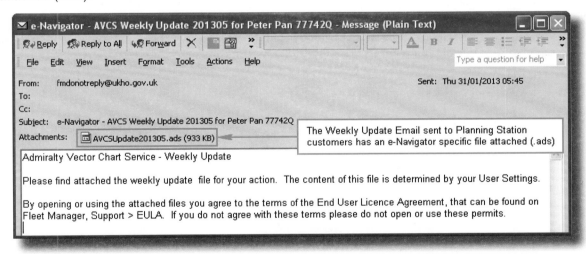

Right-click on the weekly update file (.ads) and 'Save as' to save the file in a folder. If Planning Station is not installed on a communications PC, you will need to save the file on a removable drive for transfer between computers.

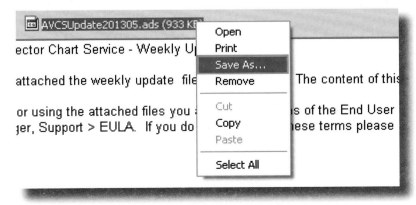

Go to Planning Station and ensure that the communication method is set to 'Removable Drive' by going to User Settings>Communication Method. Then import the weekly update file by going to Tools>Apply Update.

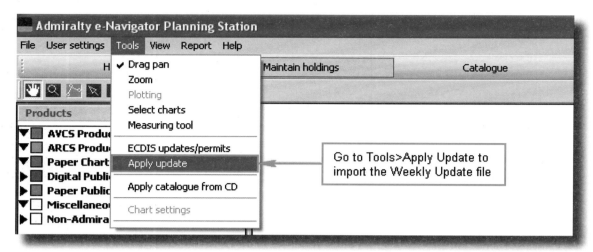

Use the 'Open' window to search for the weekly update file and double-click on the file to import.

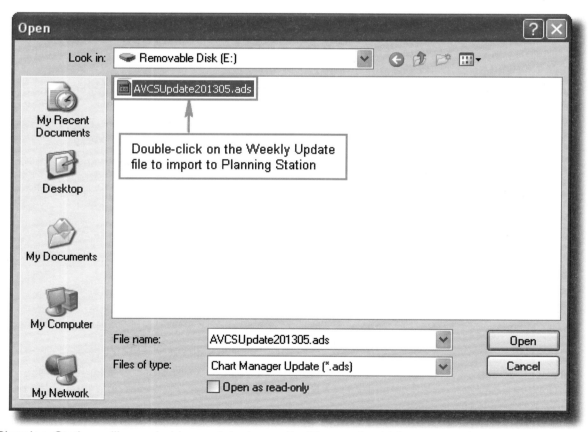

Planning Station will now hold your latest permits. These should be exported using the 'ECDIS updates/permits' wizard - See section Updating the ECDIS for details.

Receiving Data with the Weekly Update Email

Planning Station customers can choose to receive catalogues and chart data included with the Weekly Update Email. To save on download sizes, the UKHO has put in place the following controls on sending data with the Weekly Update Email:

- Update and New Chart data is only sent for products in the Working Folio
- Catalogues and data are only sent when there are changes to the AVCS or ARCS permits held, which means that a Weekly Update Email is sent
- Distributors and Shipping Companies can set restrictions on the maximum download size sent

When the Weekly Update Email is received it should be imported using the process given at the section **Applying the Weekly Update Email**. If the file contains data, a wizard will open automatically to guide you through the process of exporting the exchange set to apply to ECDIS – See section **Updating the ECDIS**.

Contact your Admiralty Distributor for more information on receiving data with the Weekly Update Email.

NOTES

NOTES

NOTES

NOTES

NOTES

NOTES

NOTES

NOTES

NOTES